Selected Poems

1953–2010

SEAGULL
BOOKS
·
CELEBRATING
40 YEARS

THE ITALIAN LIST

LUIGI DI RUSCIO

Selected Poems

1953–2010

EDITED BY MASSIMO GEZZI

WITH AN INTRODUCTION BY
MASSIMO RAFFAELI

TRANSLATED BY CRISTINA VITI

LONDON NEW YORK CALCUTTA

Seagull Books, 2023

Originally published in Italian as *Poesie scelte, 1953–2010*
by Luigi Di Ruscio
© Marcos y Marcos, 2019

First published in English translation by Seagull Books, 2023
English translation © Cristina Viti, 2023

ISBN   978 1 8030 9 158 7

British Library Cataloguing-in-Publication Data
A catalogue record for this book is available from the British Library

Cover designed by Sunandini Banerjee, Seagull Books, Calcutta, India,
using a painting by Carl Wilhelmson entitled *A Workman* from
Wikimedia Commons

Typeset by Seagull Books, Calcutta, India
Printed and bound in the USA by Integrated Books International

CONTENTS

From *The Last Collection* (2002)

From *The Laughing God* (2008)

Massimo Raffaeli

I was plunged in foetal waters,
now I am plunged in this social water.
—'Cristi polverizzati'[1] (2009)

After decades spent in a state of geographical marginality, almost a
stowaway in the publishing world (despite the support of such
exceptional guarantors as Franco Fortini, Salvatore Quasimodo,
Giancarlo Majorino, Antonio Porta), Luigi Di Ruscio's poetry broke
through like an iceberg at the turn of the millennium: that is, in the
context of a severe, systemic economico-political crisis which finally
brought out what we may, in a strict and even etymological sense,
define as that poetry's essentiality. Di Ruscio always insisted, to the
point of his voice turning hoarse, that whereas the language of power
is always a contrived, one-way fabrication, the language of the
underprivileged is upfront and direct, aiming straight and sharp for
the truth. Such language may be altered but not abjured—if any-
thing, it may be replicated through a non-negotiable, obsessive
fidelity to the primordial core of perception that legitimizes it. In
that sense, Di Ruscio has been a humanist poet in the classical

---

1 Luigi Di Ruscio, 'Cristi polverizzati' [Pulverized Christs] in *Romanzi*
(Angelo Ferracuti and Andrea Cortellessa eds)(Milan: Feltrinelli, 2014).
[Trans.]

mould since his beginnings, when at 23 he chose for his first collection a title such as *We Can't Get Used to Dying*[2]: not so much a declaration of poetics as a statement of intent and an act of resistance, willpower pitted against accepting as 'natural' the consequences of social and class dynamics. Born in Fermo[3] under the fascist regime in an alley called Vicolo Borgia, a sub-proletarian ghetto; a rebellious schoolchild who flunked out of education after primary school; an urchin running wild in the countryside; a communist with clear anarchist leanings; an odd-jobber who in 1957 emigrated to Oslo, where he spent 40 years on the shop floor of a steelwire factory—such is his *cursus honorum*, where the time of poetry, subtracted by sheer tenacity from the time of servitude, was the only privilege granted to him by what he sarcastically termed 'the social-democratic paradise'. The adventures of this time were narrated by Di Ruscio in late prose works such as *Palmiro* (1986) and *La neve nera di Oslo* (2010), true picaresque novels, autobiographical transcriptions on the border of docufiction: an extensive diversion into the comical and the grotesque, where retracing the trajectory of a personal Bildungsroman in fact means sequencing the genome of poetry's irrepressible calling. For Di Ruscio, to ask how a man becomes a man is equivalent to asking how and why a man becomes a poet. And that is why, beyond all obvious labels, he was not a 'worker-poet' or a 'poet-worker' but simply someone who through poetry was able to inscribe the workers' condition into the human condition as such.

---

2 Luigi Di Ruscio, *Non possiamo abituarci a morire* (Franco Fortini introd.) (Milan: Schwarz, 1953). [Trans.]

3 A town in the Marche region of central Italy, on the site of a proto-Etruscan settlement and later a Roman colony. [Trans.]

Rigid limits always circumscribed his writing, which mostly happened at sundown, in an eighth-floor flat in the near outskirts of Oslo (Åsengata 4C), in a room that, borrowing a term from his beloved Giordano Bruno, he would call his 'stable': a den heaped high with papers, dominated by the noisy hammering of his old Olivetti typewriter. Nobody in his family (not his wife Mary or their four children) understood Italian; nor did any of his workmates in the factory even imagine he was a writer: but it is precisely this condition of 'double partiality' (social subalternity, geo-linguistic alienation) that grants his poetry the hallmark of an accomplished whole. For Di Ruscio, to be 'down' and at the same time 'outside' meant being unable to exist anywhere but on that ever-renewed page. He was free of any ballast or baggage, and even though extremely well read, he would continue to proclaim his ignorance, mentioning among his very few early reference points Ungaretti's fragmented lyrics and Pavese's *Lavorare stanca*.[4] Although he spoke the dialect of Fermo more than Italian, he read other languages, translated Ibsen's verse from Norwegian, delved into philosophy, in particular the classics of dialectic thought, and derived from Hegel's lectures on aesthetics the definite idea that poetry corresponds to a destructured consciousness whose reversed logic commands a vitally immediate language capable of truth, and hence a much higher expressive charge than the opposite state of 'good' consciousness. This is why each one of Di Ruscio's poems potentially encloses all of his poetry, giving his entire production[5] the circular character of an authentic

4 Cesare Pavese, *Lavorare stanca* [Work Is Tiring] (Florence: Solaria, 1936). [Trans.]

5 From his first chapbook through to *Apprendistati* [Apprenticeships] (Ancona: Gilberto Bagaloni Editore, 1977), *Istruzioni per l'uso della repressione* [Repression: A User Manual] (Milan: Savelli, 1980) to the sapiential articles of *L'iddio ridente* [The Laughing God] (Tuscany: Editrice Zona, 2008).

epic. He did, in fact, state on several occasions that his *oeuvre* is shaped like the cosmos as imagined by Bruno and Spinoza: a universe whose centre is found everywhere and whose boundaries cannot be seen anywhere. Furthermore, Di Ruscio's poetic cosmos is a dynamic whole in perpetual movement—where nothing is certain except the fury of rhythm—in a stream of variations, amendments, amputations springing from an idiosyncratic orthography (distorted forms, metaplasms, coins, dialect expressions, vintage *lapsus*) that must remain in its fiery, molten state until writing (*scrivere*) becomes synonymous with inscribing (*iscrivere*). This is the maximum capacity of an implacable language that finds no respite (let alone any *ne varietur* rigidity) anywhere, not even in this definitive volume of poems selected by the author and meticulously edited by Massimo Gezzi, a scholar and poet who, like Di Ruscio, hails from Fermo.

Di Ruscio—and this is extremely unusual for a poet who started out in the mid-1900s—eschews metaphor as an ambiguous or mendacious fabrication, relying instead with irreducible insistence on metonymy. Adjectives are suspect, the poem's life force lies in nouns and verbs, its core unit is the full sentence or, rather, the web of coordinate clauses within a period. Which probably means that, for this poet, expression is intrinsic to thought, and poetry, if it is anything at all, is thought in action. Almost free from punctuation, Di Ruscio's poetry is shorn of rhetorical figures, except for repetition and inversion: the most schematic, or, we might say, the most dialectical of such devices. Verses are long, the measure is free and given momentum by rhythm—which in turn means that metrics is ultimately overridden by the pulse of prosody. The dominant pronoun is the 'I' of lyrical poetry, expanding into the 'we' of the epic—certainly not through the overheated rhetoric of 'engagement', but through the poet's sense of closeness, of literally breaking bread, with his fellow men: those sacrificed on the altar of wars dictated by power, those who have no homeland left, those who are migrants or subaltern workers toiling on the shop floor, those humiliated and silenced by the murderous exclusion/inclusion binary decreed by so-called opulent or neo-capitalist societies. In this poetry, the crucible of a sound-proofed present holds the raw material of a constant shuttling between Vicolo Borgia (flashbacks of offended life, images of suffocation and anonymity deep in remote memory) and the daily contact, made indecent, normal or entirely 'natural' by time, with the exploitation that makes each man a wolf unto the next man. Recall how half a century ago Quasimodo had thought young Di Ruscio's poetry best situated in a Hobbesian context, in the jaws of a modern Leviathan—or, as we might say today, in the vice of a no less ravenous ordoliberal society. Reading Di Ruscio—who from the lowly station of the proletarian loved to repeat with Joyce that we don't have a snowball's chance in hell—is an antidote to the 'pensée unique' liberalism that anoints a hubristic planetary hegemony: as in 'CCCXIV' (see p. 209 in this volume), where the particular and the universal fuse through a short-circuit of history and geography: 'the factory is the last station / if you get sacked it's like you've been spat out into the unknown / in a fall that will not be cushioned / the steelworker is attached to something diabolical / the Polish man says working / for the red new dawn under the communists was even worse / some of the stopped machines look like coffins / for those who are really sick / to stay off sick is not that easy / this for-eigner this Italian guy we don't know much about him / all we know is he stinks & he exists'.

So it is good that a poet who has too long been as if reserved to 'happy few' authors and scholars (most recently Eugenio De Sig-noribus, Enrico Capodaglio, Biagio Cepollaro, Francesco Scarabicchi,

Emanuele Zinato, Andrea Cortellessa) should finally meet a wider public, and that a wider commonality should be opened for the powerful, penetrating word of this 'prehistoric proletarian', as Di Ruscio was once described, in an entirely affectionate manner, by Angelo Ferracuti, the writer who was closest to him during his lifetime. Within a social landscape that seems to have been irreversibly laid waste and then stilled by glaciation, one image shines, totally isolated, in Di Ruscio's poetry—an image where history seems to be contradicting, refuting itself to turn into nature renewed (see p. 74 in this volume): 'when in the winter landscape still in the teeth of frost / suddenly the almond tree bursts into blossom', it shines like 'scant living matter enclosed in death': that almond tree lost in the freezing depths of winter is surely a reflection of existence that still expands beyond the interdictions of class and history: the 'most fragile of flags' perhaps, but as Di Ruscio writes, the flag of poetry itself—an early or off-season blossoming, standing naked and unarmed in its necessity.

We Can't Get Used to Dying
(1953)

I was five years old
an old woman got me to understand
why no one was sitting me on their knees
my grandma who was holding my hand did not take my side
neither did she soothe me by squeezing my hand
for this I have walked alone along rivers
water was no mirror to me
I'd go back home so as not to sleep in the dry riverbed
at that age hunger will drive you crazy
turn you into a grown man before your time
I learnt to gather
all the grasses grazed by goats
& got a taste for bitter flavours
that was my milk
& because I took my time stealing I got the best fruit
I went alone so I wouldn't be found out
dogs didn't bark at my smell
& no one can slate me
if I soon went to work on denying god
on the walls swollen with water
I'd seen nothing but paper images
I discovered books in the heap of the rag & bone man
I'm still spellbound looking at them
amid all the papers I was searching for the written page
I have cried out and they have seen me as a living being
something more than a wayfarer

I have gone into the streets
what child doesn't dream of dressing as a man
I became one early
I was still wearing shorts when I found
a woman & made her happy
because men gave her pain
I've glided in flight over thoughts
dreaming with each leaf I saw falling
those were the restless hours
churches were good to keep cool
I ran around thirsting after women
& soon began to pay them with stolen money.
These days I can feel women's love brushing my face with its breaths
I drive my fingers hard into their greasy hair
& I got lucky nigger lips
eyes unable to rest.

I've been out of work for years
& I'm having fun reading all the posters
I might be the only one who actually reads them all through
so as to waste my time that costs me nothing
& why I was born is written on no star
not even god remembers.
I play the football pools
& ponder the famous perm bet
but by now nothing much can give me hope in miracles
the money I stake on the hope of a break
would be better blown on drink.
Every day I walk to the job centre
today two women signing on again
were told by way of consolation
it's easier for them
they can always find work as housemaids.
Later I went to the park & stayed there till night
a couple were kissing
I too had a woman on that seat
now I have the gaze of one you might like to get
sliding from my hair to my shoes
to find me out as a tramp.
I used to go to work & cycle back home, I was so eager
I slept soundly
& partied with the woman
who I left so she'd always be waiting

now it's insomnia till daybreak
& then nightmares all the way.
I thought about ending it all
if I hold out it's from hope it will change
but I've some white strands already
without a wife & child
that's all I wish for that dream for crazy dreamers.

They breakfast on water & bread
they drink a lot of water
any spit they have must be spat out onto their hands
to stop the hammer slipping
at midday they soak up the broth of grasses
with the usual black bread
when the sun goes down if I'm full of sadness
they're happy to go back home & laugh
as they sit with the family play with the children
after ten hours' work splitting stones
for that scrap of bread & for the wife
to continue serving herself last
so no one is left without their share.

In summer the rain's good for the corn
the pigs are easier to manage
when it goes well out in the country it goes well for everyone
but in the bad season
the rain's a curse
taking cover in the shed of dry sticks
is like being outside
water streaming down your face down your shoulders
& you work like that every day
you go out on the road in the hope of getting a day's work
& the rain steals your bread
at work your spade gets muck-stuck
wheelbarrow sinking
& you've got to push lay into it with your thigh
rolled-up trousers & shins sodden through
children in the houses looking for bread
the scraps of hard bread from the days when the sun shone.

They gather snow
their hands covered in rotten blood
they put it to their mouth
for all the ice-cream
they didn't have last summer
they climb on planks of wood
& go sledging for all the dreams they didn't dream
& it will be a holiday for them too
outside their houses
holes in their clothes
wrecked-out shoes
as the snow clads the houses in frost
in this your land
where god created us bastards.

She was working as a nurse
& they sacked her & threw a few quid at her
now she's on a pension gets drunk on anisette
goes to sleep round midnight
makes herself coffee & brings me some as she sees the day break
& asks me why I write so much but never sit exams
she who sat me on her knees more than my mother ever did
she who had to dress the dead & work as a skivvy
to give me a wee bit of bread
is sick at heart to see me with nothing
she wants to have my children
& start anew as if they were hers
but it's not my fault if I was lowborn
it's not my fault—nothing is.

The pension of a town-hall clerk
sixty quid a month forty years' toil
to get bread & grated cheese
to learn to hold out his hand & die alone
or end up in the old people's home
being bossed around by the mother superior
getting up early learning to cleanse his soul
so as to have a full meal
& die in a place made for old people
to croak without bothering anyone.

He died working
eighty years spent on the job
a tin cross on his grave
a heap of soil & a number
he'd go to every single party demo
& say he'd have no priest
but paralysis
stopped him speaking.

They had syphilis
& took in a bastard, a grown girl.
She was pretty & we'd often sit together
on her doorstep without touching.
Then they got her engaged to an older guy
he was a tough case
& they say her father too had his eye
on the pretty little flesh
the hair still in plaits.
She'd got into the habit
of thinking everyone was like me.
Later she stopped understanding me.

The traffic light's red
& hangs like a god over the building site
& bicycles fly by with women in the saddle
their eyes a thousand colours
their faces stronger than death
people who savour their days
& that red on their cheeks has more light than the sun.

Over the roofs the cats are roaming
their weeping lovestruck meowings
drive minds to terror.
Bottles thrown at them out of fear.
They say that in the shadows witches buzz
& the dead rise.
I never saw anything
it's only this stark irony of mine
leads me to the ghosts
I imagine green-eyed owls
prowling in the shadow
I can see the boundless stars
& I've no fear.

Witches Wheelgrind Their Dentures

(1966)

For the pussycat in heat
toms riding on the roofs
& fun erases cracks in the house walls
the moon comes with the cock crowing
the whistling is about wanting to hush the dogs
that bark & strain as if wanting to bite
the wind that blows tonight bringing the bitches' smell
the moon slides by in the clouds its light glancing through
& what should I decide at this time of night
that never comes to an end
thoughts stick to walls & stones
witches wheelgrind their dentures on the roofs.

A church is being built for St Michael the Archangel
the angel who fought the devil down
yesterday the bishop & cardinal came to visit
only the lackeys bowed & kissed their hands
under thirty-degree heat I dream of the revolution
with all my strength I talk workers up
& into doing as little as possible
the foreman yells & measures performance in hours & metres
& says everyone is underperforming
the priest says we'll get indulgence
me, like some old hero I get downcast or elated
sometimes I think of nothing but the earth I'm digging
the bricks I'm loading
in the evening I look at the hills & think of her who loves me
on Sundays we take a day off take off to the seaside
the foreman yells in rage & decrees fines
now & again the list of redundancies
is pinned to the office door
& your thoughts are loaded with hatred
I only see my woman on Sundays
our kisses are full of lusts they've been waiting six days
that's six days too long.

They say you need to lay a soul
in the foundations before you pour the footing
instead of the usual cat they'd soon put in
the guy with a woman's voice
who complains his wife's not getting pregnant
& gets arm-broken when he lifts a full spade
& finds speaking too much of an effort
ends his words with a pipsqueak wave
& a roll of his eyes
if he does speak those listening will laugh
find funny double meanings for his crippled words
only when he's drunk will he talk fast in his woman's voice
& rant out some turn of phrase they will ape in mock falsetto
when they remind him to his face he was found unfit for duty
& if the king won't have you
no more will the queen

Pampurio

When he walks his composed figure
that looks like a character from
the kids' comic strip makes even grown-ups laugh
& yell out his nickname
he throws bricks squeezes his brain dry
to find insults meant to be offensive
that in fact just make you laugh all the more
someone tells him he shouldn't get mad
the more he does the worse they get
but he feels he's lost all the dignity
by which he's been & still is looking for a position
fascism or democracy made no odds to him
used to sell bleach now he's from the unemployment factory
only under the republic of Salò
did he get a job at the rations office
by signing up as a card-carrying fascist
but he got purged & his job given to another guy
bad liver at fifty
at work he staggers & loosens his belt.

They say if you want to know the future
you need to make a deal with angels or the devil
& this one who's been wearing a crooked face
since his right side was struck by polio
must have traded with the devil
in the block for the homeless where he lives
he'll slash bicycle tyres disconnect electric wires
almost no one goes to see him any more
to show the lines on their hands & get their fortunes told
so to stay alive he carries water on a government building site
in his early days he used to get palm-reading gigs
by telling stories of the evil one attacking him
& the forces protecting him
so he was tempted just as they tempted Christ
lay them inside the foundations
tell us how selling your soul is done
he no longer speaks of magic
he speaks of life & how it's mangled him
& moans as he walks his worn-down walk
carrying the water jug
along the road that comes out of the tall corn.

His work is the necessary offer of each day
to an unfathomable insatiable God
his life is all in this offering perhaps he enjoys it
& will do unto the last day of his weariness
the farmer planted the vineyard for him
every year the new wine froths up for him
so he receives the best offering every day
& here he is all of him in the quaking of houses
in a new lightness exploding in rage or in joy
earth made by these men who wait for the last encounter
the last sacrament the last offering over a whole lifetime's offering
brick sand gravel all loaded on his back
for the building of the Picene houses with their pastel colours
scattered along hills that yield low wine
or plains that yield the bedrock of short rivers
all the hours of his life heaped up merciless
like the gravel the river heaps up to its mouth
licked in a tireless game by men & by the sea.

In summer he eats tomatoes in winter potatoes
gets a taste of meat on canonical holidays
or at wheat or olive harvest
avoids pigs by throwing well-aimed stones at their backs
running over hay fields
he finds the nests of birds & grass snakes
lays traps along ditches for thirsty birds
in the evening he sits quiet his eyes full of sleep
hears the grown-ups talk
& holds some thoughts in his brain
olive trees are like people
they suffer from summer heat & winter northerlies
& in his half-sleep he thinks of people & olive trees
of the oil between the segments of the tomato
where he dips his sop
waving flies away wearily because it's time to sleep
he lays his head on his mother's thigh
flies can land on his head now
they've lost the quick knack of catching them in flight
& tearing off their wings so they can live on
as worms for chickens to peck up.

Her belly can't wait to be filled
her breasts to swell up with milk
she can feel the pain of the drought-stricken earth
the pain of live plants when they're struck by the frost
she's spellbound by the holiday fireworks tearing up the sky
& solemnly walks in the square with the fiancé
who would spend too much on one holiday in the year
her life's satisfied with this round of cattle & land
provenances & explanations
all already inscribed in her sky
& she lives her life honourably
the life she keeps like leading the cattle to drink
holding them fast the rope of the bit
locked around their black nostrils.

26

Against the sun he'll quench his thirst with wine
wear a straw hat decked with flowers
of the young men getting drunk he's the only one left
after the daily toil he's in the cafe till late at night
gambling at bezique & winning as the whim goes on any day
he fought the partisan war desperado style
an action was a hit like any other
he lives his life like he plays bezique
he'll only lose if he dreads getting lost.

This is the street where I struggled to find my first words
where I saw german helmets & bombs go off
gutted houses & nights swallowed by fear
images of pierced madonnas
& frightening christs blood-stained plaster
my father's harsh cigarettes their red brand red heartland shining
the breathlessness strafing my throat the grip of nausea
I grew up within these walls
that rise walled up in earth
with wall grass climbing along the cracks
with thistles by the side of the roads
where death walked whether german or allied
& there was no time to even weep for the dead
as belief struggled from darkness into matter
with the clandestine whistling of a song for the red flag.

Fifty square yards of floor & we danced
to bass drum & trumpet rhythms & the women were unstoppable
we were rough & ready with all the latest hits
speaking words full of love to one another
with each dance the women would line up together on the sides
& wait for us no man felt shy
no woman was left without a man
the women were hard some light & easily led
some others had firm thighs some soft as those who have known love
the men were playful the women beatific taking their fun
some were falling into a man's arms for the first time
some were holding a woman for the first time.

She walks in the streets
her eyes wistful with hunger
lingers long over job adverts
that speak of maidservants for sale
of women seeking husbands
of men seeking pleasant looks
& all the things for sale
& all the things for buying
but not for me & you
on the merciless town square
fill in all the applications
where they ask your name
birth details
if you're married or with children
any convictions
your skills your ideas & state of mind
calm & plain handwriting
from our wistful-headed hunger.

Maria I met on her Sunday off work
an illiterate servant but they put
a white starched cap like a crown on her head
the first time glued together in the same old cinema
then the road leading into the countryside
a glorious spring & evenings of sweet-smelling grass
together in the grass riding high
only sated in the end for new hunger
Maria the best
today like a lightning bolt you've struck
& stand square in front of me driving me blind.

We spend years with the tressette game in the evening
& words repeated over & over again about the cards we played
or walking at night
telling each other what's deepest inside us
thinking of the future as thieves might think of their plans
we discuss the world look for the proof of existence
now & again one of us leaves on brightly-lit liners
some others as volunteers or immigrant miners in Belgium
& those who didn't get thousands of sea miles
or weren't gobbled up by the coal mine
will come back as soldiers do
with a suitcase full of sorrow
some others go to Rome carrying a letter
of introduction to a notable or member of parliament
who will swap that letter with another letter
& they sleep in the dosshouse eat bread & dust
start over the next day walk all over this drunken dazed Rome
the others keep walking all over their hometown any which way
recalling the names of constellations.

You'd learnt to smoke before all the others
fouling up your mouth with smoke your fingers with nicotine yellow
you were the gang leader with the names of the slowest animals
when invading troops flooded our villages
you'd wait for drunken soldiers outside the tavern
& filch their wallets bulging with colourful notes
you turned into a monkey
to get into the camp tents & steal
so we could get a bellyful of meat
& get drunk with endless smokes
now your life continues in the lands of Australia
where you'll carry on honing your cardsharp skills
& you might come back even though no one ever should
better be content with carrying in their wallets
soiled prayer cards with their patron saints' pictures
because with the homecoming even the saints
become the same old statues of painted wax
through the hometown flooded with bright adverts
a new war is raging
made of debt traffics newly rich newly bankrupted people
& among the death notices
the posters of actresses with their long long thighs
you'll find new reason
new games to shoot down the blues
along the reedbeds here are the new houses
of a fat smug populace

no one'll recognize you you'll no longer recognize
anything not even the two of us who will recognize each other
the two of us who spent our whole childhood playing together
we'll not find our memories even.

Everywhere the last
for this hideous race of me-firsts
the last in his homeland a tenner for a day's work
the last in this new land
owing to his Italian voice
the last one left with his hatred
& you'll be branded one & all by the hatred of this man
un-nailed & crucified anew with each hour
damned for a world of the damned.

Over here no one man ever met another
everything's walled up inside one & the same gesture
voiceless objects reappearing only to disappear again
each word is the same word
each figure spells doom for the other
what obsessed pieceworker relentlessly manufactures you
what derangement creates the repetition of the same figure
where have they come from all equal to the point of spasm
how will the choice be made the saved told apart from the lost
what subtlest one will be able to tell you apart
& look at you as if it were possible to find inside your steps
something carrying the echoes of faraway discoveries
—to spin around in this world
where every gob of spit is subject to authorization
learning to look when travelling on a tram
for the seat farthest from what's meant to be my fellow man
I've learnt to wall my mouth in like a wound
& spy the cracks in your faces.

Even if after the toil my brain
is still under the sway of the furious building work
that has me build nails
without ever knowing who they'll crucify
after a little rest a meal
the same fury has me pound words onto the keys
has you drum out signs & compact colours
& we can still chain up the monsters
overcome & digest them for the night for our joy
in the chaos of your house
where your wife & daughter & dinner wait for you
after lifting your cutlery as if you were lifting tools
& me in my three-by-five room
white walls & thousands of white sheets
to nail me to the cross & crucify me
fighting the tiredness the dirt
& everything is still next to us
don't wait for Saturdays the beginning of God's rest
let rest still be far away
let rest still be for God
& this hell for us.

Six a.m. the start of our day
we are the start of every day
the round of the hours begins
on the draw bench that waits for me with her mouth wide open
my dance begins, my show
at certain hours of the day
clear sunlight enters the shop floor
& for a short while our dirt
is cleared as in the saints' images
I steal a moment for a smoke that scrapes my throat
like a thief I watch the minutes on the big eye of the clock face
thoughts chasing thoughts a play-acting show chasing another
then as we reckon up each instant inside one blessed instant
the wail of the siren comes to shake us
rest awaits & tomorrow's wake-up call
the alarm bursting into our dreams blasting them away
and on like this every day of my existence
in good spirits out of my wits.

Eight hours multiplied by a whole lifetime
covering the courage of heroes & all saints
interchangeable men dancing men
the machine is our soul
the clock-in card
holds the dates of our history
production is our logbook
scraping up all clownish cover-ups
all of our soul locked between four revolting walls
where the God of the year two thousand croaks in perpetuum
& is in perpetuum reborn
each of our days for this God that's our own voice
the God that's in our hands
the God milled & welded every day
& there's nothing more spellbinding
than this fury coming to a halt
seized by a mortal paralysis
the stopped machine a throat-slit mammoth
the strike ballot passed in the union meetings
a stop to the God
& to his driver & the earth shakes
the stopped factory
spreads the dread of doomsday around the earth
& if clocking in is our verb today
the day of our victory is held back & we are
living for this day
living for this wait.

My Father & the Ants

The day I found my father looking at the ants
the sun was splitting stones & stunning the bricklayers who wore
    no paper hats
a dark hole & pellets of clotted soil around it
& the teeming of the ants dragging seeds too big for their mouths
& my father in disgust scraped his foot over the anthill
it was so that I learnt to look at ants with this disgust
the only human thing about my father is this abstract disgust
this nothingness assaulting the senses & my father drowning it
in the card games with broad beans as chits
& greeting every win or loss with wine
& the binge bringing out a sort of desperate fury
& he smashes plates & glasses against the wall
& dooms himself in his fury & stopped-up mouth
& in the toil a doomed battle without purpose or sense
my father has found his own image in the ant & destroys it
the wine the toil the smoke smash through his chest at night
with a frightening cough that has always been there through all of
    our sleeps
he destroys his life every day with a long series of years
that are too strong to be destroyed too early
this bad habit of watching the ant has doomed my father
he lives on this earth in perfect rancour
& everything has become perfectly useless to my father
what's left is the binge stopped in his throat the fury attacking
    his brain

& so I too get desperate at the ant
I live on this anthill & learn to destroy myself with rage
because all I have left of so many flags
is my father in his disgust crushing the hard-working ant.

Holy Week

The priests sweat in the rites
of crucifixes in purple palls
so that we will in good order
get to the day when symbols are revealed
the spear the sponge on the cane the withered crown
the pierced ribcages
the foreheads drippling with blood
inside their sealed glass cases
peas & broad beans shall split open
& the sharp smell of vegetables
will initiate children's capers in oat fields
the raw almond shall flood mouths with sharpness
the tied-up bells will peal out madly on the Saturday
red sheaves of tulips will be gathered
in the wheat fields with their blinding green
nature wide open & happy the girl who today
discovers her fledgling down her first menstrual blood
the boy has picked the highest tuft of oat
& now lays traps for the lizard
peeping out of holes in the walls
nothing more delicately precise
than the gesture of one who waits outside the den
ready to seize the monstrous animal
the black water snake along the ditches
creates curvy moves & will seize the toad
soon they'll be filling bottles of water with tadpoles

& they'll see this fullness of life shaded from the sun
the earth is spinning time round in wide circles
& those who are saved will be saved for us all
noble beetles shall be strung along slender threads
& in good order shall fly around your head.

In the days of the passion in 1944
the Internationale already seething its songs inside him
he kissed Christ's spat-upon feet for the last time
waiting for the plaster Christ to come un-nailed
in a once & for all easter
his childhood games consisted
of raising your altar on cardboard boxes
water and crusts of bread for your body & blood
as gospel the latest issue of the adventure comics
where Flash Gordon & Mandrake
raised him to dreams of the highest
too soon the war
had him close the missals & shut off this altar
too soon he left the confession-box games
where he kept accurate tally of his masturbations
so as to be able to open his mouth with a clear conscience
& stretch out his tongue to receive all the first Fridays in the month
all the Sundays in the week
his father stitched clandestine leaflets into his jacket lining
& his eyes found new adventures
new enthusiastic outbursts
perhaps Mandrake was in the sign of the swastika
Flash Gordon in the tiger tanks the war patrols
in their goose-stepping ranks
as they climbed up the retreat paths
seeding the underbridges with gunpowder packs

you too O Christ must have been with them
the door was not locked when ranked
with the black shirts as young fascists or clowns in mourning
as his father would say they came to look for you
knives at their belts dwarf guns at shoulder-arms
these too were his games
that he packed up calmly in the days of passion
to run after flags that flew with brighter colours
back then they'd kill one another for this as well
to ring the changing of the guard
exchange a flag for a new flag
that would allay his father's bolshevik fury.

The sun has bowed out behind the hills chunks of blue amid black
    cirrus
the north wind swoops on the town
the copper cockerel vanes on the cathedral screech on their pivots
the wind swoops on window frames the howls on the roofs
gusts of paper dust & cigarette butts rise up & race along the ground
this evening the neurasthenic will have a headful of shouts
lust lording it over him his thoughts running headlong
the dirty dusty wind blowing into any place to spy on anything
I'm holding fast onto the hundreds of bottles at this counter
holed up in this cafe in the town centre my pockets full of newspapers
scraps of paper the last proletarian poem the last receipt
& the small change I rattle in my pocket
the door opens he lowers his coat collar as he comes in
I can see his face very well now about to open his mouth
a hoarse stalinist juventus supporter with a wallet full of cards
communist political-refugee peace-partisan card
department-of-work card unemployment card
sports correspondent-for-l'unità-third-series card
& ID card DOB 1921
not very tall at all but red hair
his father an anarchist his maternal & paternal uncles anarchists
a whole anarchist generation
purged coshed interned for having at their funeral
the black & white triangular anarchist flag
their names in police files for almost a hundred years

the files passed down from father to son
& at the time of Salò all of them in the mountains
red neckerchief with the communists waiting for the day of anarchy
each an anarchist in his own way a libertarian communist
individualist anarchist & the last in the series a sports communist
in charge of press releases & propaganda
so many cards & so much ancestry to end up sitting here unqualified at
        a bar counter
we stick our tongues into our coffee cups
the national brand cigarette comes undone gets black sticks to your lips
we close our right eyes they're fouled up with smoke & shed tears.

On this day more rain chucking itself down at the earth
houses & streets washed bright like worms & take a good look at this
     town square
where I have listened open-mouthed to the oratorical voices
clapping my hands raw getting inflated & deflated
the balcony of the house of fascism with the last fascist in a black shirt
& a partisan with a red neckerchief slapping him around
I could hear the smacks ringing onto my face I was seeing red
the window of the house of fascism on its last day
puking furniture & papers onto the paving stones
a flurry of documents fluttering about
with the pigeons who had survived the war
so many pretty women have ridden these stones
so many times I have opened your mouths sniffed the air spying
at every corner
to see if anything might change
if at least one of the prophecies might come true
this is where I listened in a daze
in my young-fascist uniform to the Duce's voice
my teacher hitting me in the face with the Giornale d'Italia
pissed off with my thunderstruck expression my dirty uniform
no one but him on the balcony of the house of fascism
the loudspeaker blaring
& then like a hand laying a curse
the sound of the big cathedral bell spreading around the arcades
walking around this square is no mean feat these days

all of me right out there to be sized up
all of my lusts laid out in the open.

Not everyone can smell the blood of a butchered pig
but the pig can sense his own death
& it took four of them to hold him down
as they slid the knife between his ribs
& the blood-choked grunt will stay with you
the blood steamed as it clotted
& my father stood with a basin
to gather it as if under a fountain
once clotted it will be cooked with chunks of lard
a meal that tastes like sand stops up your stomach
& leaves your mouth feeling like it's been stuffed with soil
they took wide leaves as trays for the heart
the lungs innards & brains
there was a commandment against feeding on blood
we don't aspire to any prescribed salvations
stuck with our filths we carry them on our backs.

The Fountain of the Bishop's Palace

Few things have given me so much pleasure as drinking this water at night
feeling its matter as it dissolves dullness & cleanses your mouth
the tongue struck by the sudden chill writhing around the teeth
& the tastes of hell & brimstone stuck down in the throat
in my childhood years I'd wake up after furious sleeps
my eyelids stuck together with yellow gunk
my grandmother would take that water & melt away the wake-up blindness
the eye looks up & is clear now it might be because as they say
those who drink of this water will always have clear sight
the big spurt comes out the mouth of a stone head
an Assyrian mug with eyes like goose eggs
symmetrical hair in womanly curls
the face of enigma when bending under that stone face
I take my night drink
among patrician houses silent as dens of thieves
a fountain stuck into the huge wall
of the bishop's palace with its archive files of every sin
& every punishment to be suffered by every man
over here by the time one bishop dies five popes have croaked
governments topple-turned memorial stones smashed in
the night has the same impassive face
the fountain vein keeps spurting in its calm even flow
old people used to say it was the devils' water
that swelled the fountain of the wholesome eye
in this land each stone has a story to tell
the fountain pisses its water out

& my head sails around in it
in this August of holiday homecomings
of classless people like beggars
lickers of hallowed stones.

The hearse was filing down a road
that in June was as if buried in ripe wheat
the haymakers would stand & look
whetstone blows sharp on the scythe's edge
for fifty years the same coach driver has ferried
the dead of this town of firmest faith
to the rest that knows no tiredness
black horses polished with iron bristles
the crusts of scurf & dried sweat
falling off into endless scales
& it was wonder at this animal
who could stand up even when asleep
with veins swollen & throbbing as if filled with acids
& eyes like the holy ghost's
wedged into the equinelateral triangle
these ferries for dead people were the last horses left in the town
the stable men put on black uniforms
men & uniforms gave off the same horsey stench
the last remnant of a human conglomeration
that only death enclosed by now
& the wailings were a need to escape death they did not crack
the bit of glass on certain deluxe coffins
where for the last time you could glimpse
a face already turning black
or lost in a vertigo of whiteness
no dearth of holy water spurting out

& finally the plaque 'to the departed peace in God'
& here come the numberless crosses
the ceramic photographs
I counted each moustache
there were all sorts of moustache
& so many young smiles in the photographs
as if they were keepsakes for your sweetheart
the noise of gravel of the mourners' march
it was necessary to at least close your eyes
stay out of the party thrown for those lined up in the burial vaults
filed away in ranks of grim elegance
death was the last show
the priest was trying to fulfil & absolve.

I can't find any of you none of you & as if in contrition remember you
now that I'm settled & in the doghouse I'm waiting
for those who'll come to meet me again
I've found this hole to dig & dig it diligently
at night I try to set my breath to my wife's
& of all the things I hear very few can get me going
my wife who's got pregnant can't wait for
her belly to open she feels all of life's movements
that's my child already stirring from inside the belly.

Jailed in these dazed streets
I'm walking & carrying my mouth out in the open
on this day erased from the calendar
I'm carrying myself around a written page for every hour
the rigmarole words crash together in splendid mechanisms
I cling to whatever strikes me
I live inside this struggle filled with hideous layers of silence
each like a king with his despair
even the moon is laughing at so many words to say nothing
& looks at the miracle of these mouths
that open to make noise
I've no talking to cast spells on things
no ghosts to jump on me
I have this poverty of gestures that are not matched by anything
& my leap into the spate of this terror
for the clarity of one word left unsaid
one gesture not made
one man unpredicted
instead I have these unfermented remnants
mountains of bones calcified by sanitations
foodstuffs precious flowers
for our life plunged to the lowest share value.

I can't stand it any more sharing my meals with you
sharing my sleep my work with you
end where you end
live through what you live through
will I have to wait for death
before what's meant to happen does happen?
now the alarm machine-guns my minutes against the empty night
am I waiting for what won't happen tomorrow?
now that everything's shot through with the fever of mobilization
& everything works to turn us into the clowns of collective desires
now that as an individual I'm under threat
& my figure is lost among all the figures
now that I wear out my brain for no use
to find the formula of my person
now that I can't find anything I don't have in anyone else
or anyone else in me
& breathing the same air as you
makes me lose myself in you
& hating you is hating myself
& I compare myself to stones to water
& if I'm alive my brain's submerged
the words I write I fish them out
crouched back into myself I write this page
it's like tracing the lines for the map
of a useless continent.

I'm busy repenting for sins I've not committed
this game of morra with no more shouted numbers
I'm busy checking all the visions
& for each object I set aside an image
which God shall I have to embrace
to live in harmony with myself
to shake off these bouts of rage
deranged around these streets among latest-model people
cinerama nature & birds in perfect tune
I kiss my woman & my mouth is trademarked
& you plaster Christ you should have come to be messiah now
we'd have heard your voice by turning the radio dial
we'd have seen your torture on eurovision
I can no longer live in this blinding air
in these slaughtered streets beyond my fellow man
in my room that I could well mistake for any of the others
if I didn't have the street name & number in my pocket
with my face melting into all these faces
by now there's only a few things keep me alive in myself
but at the cost of spending my life in perfect rancour
I fight in hatred for the uniqueness of this my life
this water stain on the wall of my room
that is only for me the image of splendid battles of angels.

In this sunshine lighting up the day in solid hours
with happiness stopping my throat
I enter these daytimes of love
& you my companion are my blinded day
the blood seems to flow in wider circles & renew me
& I love everything today now that brightness
is spun out into an endless day
today I am capable of loving every man
I love every woman tenfold
all the women I see a hundredfold
the woman who sleeps with me today a thousandfold
I love everything everythingfold
the actions in my day I relish them
relish each & every thing I consume
while my brain in its splendid levities
happily whirls with monsters
in the holy playing of the eternal game.

Time passes in front of the white pages
in a silence only scratched by my pen
as the festive firefly weaves her happy dance
on the deep faraways of night
I find my happiness in tunnelling deep
with you all behind my back in your childish & motherly sleeps
lying gently in clear dreams of linear consciousness
as people with nothing to regret not now not ever
I blow my cover in this practice every night
so I can live with you & have nothing left hidden.

The hard-earned days are piled up like new heaps of manufactured products
carefully counted & ledgered by serious accountants
time beats on all the neighbourhoods in the planet
& brings us news of fear
all the resolutions for which I do time on this unhinged machine
spitting out its tiny parts
you can die by the hand of a private killer
or wheelground from a malignant cancer
but the Spaniard can escape these unpredictable deaths
in Spain you croak at the hands of the filthy garrotte
in the name of Franco the Christian the killer
the days of general butchery are leaping up in front of us
the days of state murder
mantled in flags & ideals
this day born from the depth of fear
& we contemplate the killers' leftovers
this gash of tearing pain
slashing our mind with its reminder of the hideous law
if a man is a killer
it's because the killer
is still lurking in each one of us.

This is also a Christ
whose skin & testicles are being torn off today
to make him talk smash open his walled-up mouth
newspapers all over the planet broadcast the photographs
of the torn apart the raped
& those who have kept silent for six million Jews
are still silent & if their mouths open it's to scream
crucify the son of man so that the beast will live
so that the filthy feast can carry on beyond these blocks
where the human ant lives on locked in
beyond this Christ locked in the ciborium
blinded so he can descend
into a Pilate who washes his hands
& will carry on washing them
until they're torn off of him.

What It Means to Be a Poet

In front of the typewriter as in front of a shrine
I've tried to build rigorous pages
the way you pave a street stone upon stone
mired in every contradiction
I used to look for my verse on tram rides
my head stuck to the window glass dazed & disgusted
verse mangled into murky grooves & tongues ready to burst into secret
    resentments
I used to look for answers all of them in this night-time write-out
finally understanding not much salvation is to be found in this loosening
    of papers
in this search for the sentence you'll repeat like a prayer till tiredness
    comes
waiting as you wait for grace to blurt out something new & unexpected
running around with poems like passports well stuck to your skin
each sheet ready to leap out like a flag unfurled
all the colours of dreams analysed in delirium
all my steps measured
the real anguish & the many imaginary ones were all given names
keep up your morale amid literary pigswills
calling God's name
even though you believe any prayer to be useless
hammering this typewriter
in an exercise that keeps me in good spirits
baring yourself on sheets of paper to be itemized
into huge indices like registry office ledgers

the shapeless filthy dimension of the ridiculous ape
the chained parrot the blind canary
throw yourself into the new avant-gardes
& tell tangled little tales to cast profound spells of banality
all life in this exercise of swerving well-fed animals
building wonky word castles
where fuckwit good cheer is the rule
puking up words without stopping until the paper ends
all shame confessed
all little altars defiled
they've put the camera in front of God
& snapped him in dirty poses
may be best to go back to rhyming & make each one of our
    drivellings pretty
embrace western faiths in front of the holy ghost
if we become holy-water poets we'll not even get killed
the priest will see us to the grave
well content with blessing our souls.

He was unwell & complaining
his wife gave him sugared water to make him better
& he died then they dressed him the doctor came the priest came
& for a whole day you could hear the litanies
later that day his soldier son came
he was the only one who wept
the next day before the sun was high
four men took the body
put him in the zinc box
placed the box in the alley
welded the zinc shut as the litanies were said
people were looking down from the windows
damned if there was one crying
like when he was born damned if there was one smiling
they painted acid onto the zinc with a cockerel feather
they were working on a dead thing by now
in the church they said mass
then down into the ground with his headstone.

He used to drink gingerly like a boy
& he died his head smashed onto the pavement
messed up with engine oil petrol & blood
well dressed despite his age
had a good head for figures
& was able to get love his face was so bright
but despite his good memory he was walking weird
that's why the dead accountant was dead wrong
& despite the death notices speaking
of a life spent doing good
he died like a damned soul with no last rites
& no dignity spilling out globs of brain.

For Giuseppe Morichetti

In the alley of the virgins in the ravings of childhood fevers
barrels were rolling & the barrels hit against the town walls
then I came back to that street for the books you would lend me
& to show you the poems that came out in constant tides
you'd point your thin intellectual finger at the pages with calm irony
& told the wrong lines apart from the ones that now astonish me
then life became easy for me you would meet me happy & satisfied
the verses took up the trash heaped up inside my consciousness
to plunge it into the endless depths of this short life
in your room with the madonna of tears now in pride of place
her face stunned & the seven swords piercing her motherly breast
books were piling up in the sideboards
& you'd choose the one that would open or enrich the inner self
& my reading was frantic
as if meant to sate a long-standing long-walking hunger
each act comes full circle only the trash comes back to the surface
memory has the power to find the unfinished
the variance hue that brings me a chain of images
sure I'll still be able to capture the span of a chain of arches
but the barrels were rolling only in my dreams
the barrelman works on a different street
further away he's hammering the staves together
& the blows ring out.

When they found the spy & shot him
& down on the ground he was scratching away
you puked & that puke was your courage
in that scrap of soil drenched in blood
there were no home countries or ideals left
only your disgust for that death
administered like a sacrament
later even in our night-time roamings
we'd find ourselves in front of the graveyard wall
stick our fingers between bricks to find the holes
this is where other hands killed a man
who'd cut the telephone wires
he was walking home with the wires coiled over his shoulder
sure he'd earned the day
they killed him quick just one burst
one hammer blow just one to bang the nail down
so we began to talk of leaving for a country
where the mashinpistol holes might have been whitewashed
where the names in graveyards are none of our business
tired of walking these streets
where we saw the undertaker lurking everywhere
ready to dig our grave
the graveyard wall we've seen it well
kiss mothers and fathers wipe our mouths
leave these feasts for other feasts other hopes.

The earth is scorched like a chimney flue
the vine shoots have cracked open
the corn grains are boiled white
the scarecrow walks with his head of burnt straw
life is splashing about in the river
in the water that strands into mud
where he crawls & bare-handed grabs the slippery eel
that gives it up its head smashed onto the stone
the pike with its hellish mouth bites & dies hissing
today he learnt to catch fish with the sharp fork
he throws it into the water that rushes over his writhing catch
if he can't throw himself into the same water today
one lucky shot is enough
for his weapon with its three sharp prongs
to come back with a spiked prey
the birds fly with thirsty open mouths
the only sound they've been throwing out since daybreak is squeaky glass
you need only lay a net on the side of a bit of water
to bring back a game bag full of feathers
the peasants in the churches
pray the saints specialized in hot weather
in preparation for the atonement procession
where the guys from the brotherhood will shake their sticks & their christs.

He walked lame carrying knotty canes
screamed out curses against God & fascism
felt women's breasts in the crush of festival throngs
& never was a hand raised against him
to hush that one voice coming up from the madness of syphilis.
When they smashed all the fascist stone plaques
his sudden fury flared up frightening
& the rotten one shook his stick & screamed out
'Italians you forked tails'
all the fascist images the brass symbols
were hurled into the sewers or onto the roofs
& they rushed out towards the new symbols
& those legs with chunks of concrete
were walking as if forever liberated
out of dark mazes
their dark sexes rotting through
breaking through their flesh.

Enunciations
(1993)

1

the planet shines at its splendid brightest
the time of darkness is about to plunge to its end
we'll see the sun move into the constellation of capricorn
we'll see the asteroid shoot across the pride of planets
the asteroid will rush past among dead planets
joy in all this despair
the endless depths with fireflies & their heartbeats
to be the least possible to leave a bird's imprint on the snow
birds' imprints in the air so light in their birdlike lightness
in this trembling world now at the end
of its multiplications of frogs & grasses
the water (multiplication in this world) the water

2

when in the winter landscape still in the teeth of frost
suddenly the almond tree bursts into blossom
early extreme fragility of your splendour
the threat hangs over you the early ones are in mortal danger
the almond tree shines as it blossoms our most fragile of flags
you flag of early death & of all beginnings
scant living matter enclosed in death
our most fragile signs of hope about to end
early shoots of a new world & so splendidly alive
throat gripped tight by death

3

the spirit flooded me with light especially when I was running
the joy of love was swallowing me whole
we were flooded with light then chaos came then night & darkness
a happy angel chosen among the best sprinters was following me
with long long wings he whooshed me into relentless disquiet
of certain years I only remember the brightness of the sun
& a happy rain hammering on corrugated iron
& I had everlasting days at my disposal
& a silence only scratched by my pen
while the festive firefly weaves her happy dance
on the edge of night's plunging depths
all was animated with each mouthful of air breathed in
& no return will be needed
all is forever incarnated
I'll have everything before my eyes
with the same lucid torn-apart joy

4

I get up at five in the morning
the day starts like nothing's the matter
I keep writing until everything's as easy
as the relentless shortening of shadows
everything's easy as vertigo
to write one verse so as to write them all
to brush against all deaths for the one death
(writing as the supreme attempt to be exposed
without being seen) & I was thinking that on that town square
where in certain hours of the day
the exposure of the underwritten yourstruly was total
not even the eternalfather would have found me
all is playful mystery sweetest vulva
the mild clean sweetness of this instant
is that I can write for a whole hour
after the first notion everything writes itself calmly
& it would be so easy to finish by jumping out the window
so that the poem is seen in the final flight
clearer & clearer until the final smash-up
we deem ourselves guilty of the sum total of all enjoyments
unto the end of all verb & all flesh

6

man is descended from monkeys or pigs
your eye is porcine
& my work at the draw bench is that of an exact monkey
the war for internationalism & communism
is long & terrifying
just like the long & terrifying life of a steelworker
& one day they'll say
we are descended from exact worker apes
who over centuries despite the workers' brutish fatigue
led a series of struggles & conspiracies
hurling flags into the mire
picking them back up from the mire
engaging in a series of reckless
& perfectly reckoned struggles
one worker's skeleton will appear
in the museum of industrial civilizations
another will end up in the horror
of London's anthropology museum

8

when I suddenly come across one of my poems again
it seems to me I'm reading it for the first time
& everything is repeated & joywhirls into frightening vortexes
or when Adrian suddenly runs up to meet me
I've the very strange feeling I'm seeing
my three-year-old self tottering up to meet me
& everything is before language
the clearer & sharper the impression
the more faltering & stammering the verse
an impossible task
like describing your own death throes

9

in these 1980s
I imagine I can write poems like it's 1953
the sharecroppers still screaming against the new land agreements
armed with a pair of theatre binoculars I was peering into Jupiter's satellites
I'm peering into a cosmoagony or so I used to say
despite hope flying all over the place
& me living almost entirely
in that hope—light & flyaway as I was
(it's easy to train pigs all you need
is pocketsful of potato peelings)
I saw the last dirigible flying calmly across our air
not used to seeing the unusual I was seized by panic
hell burns & gives no light burns & darkens
(*ardet et non lucet*)
& poetry as illumination is not possible
unless we're all in the dark

11

suddenly I see everything as happy
in this insignificance piling up
all these bad-news thoughts I travel through in my half-sleeps
& if the thermonuclear catastrophe breaks out it will spare
the farthest places in Greenland the Eskimos will once again be
  masters
of their frozen land eyes of otters or whales
huge oranges full of live vitamins
I was reviewing all the most miserable peoples on earth
where on earth will the riches of the thermonuclear catastrophe be
  scattered
not even colds will migrate any more
cancer cells multiplying wildly
to defend all sorts of pride & class exploitation too
we're capable of destroying every man
to defend class pride & exploitation
milk from the motherly breasts full of radioactive isotopes
no one was who they thought they were
they swore death to one another & still we could sleep peacefully
until we heard strange noises (she was pregnant)
the doctor found out the foetus had hiccups (sobs & weeps)
we'd start awake with those internal sob-hiccups
(the foetus is seized by the hiccups or else is sobbing & weeping)
the messages warning of impending catastrophe
were not always perceived
despite everything being sunk deeper & deeper in anguish

13

as I spoke to a born-blind man
of all that I could see
I got a better view of this hideous world
hideous laughing happy world
I got a better view
of long eternal threeternal centuries of plunder
& I shall be devoured
because of the limits of my temporal condition
the blind man kept being blind
& the guardian angel also fell
his fallen flight heavy as lead

15

the rapporteur had been rapporteuring all day
late that night he was seized by tiredness headaches toothaches
he was smoking desperately didn't manage to speed up
& keep up with the discussion as it unfolded at a frightening pace
even an immigrant back home for the holidays wanted to discuss
even some who hadn't been invited wanted to discuss
because the steering committee was too tired
with all those toothaches it could no longer steer a thing
they'd often go to the bar sharp short coffees cognac anisette
even some of those who were not present wanted to discuss
the tables began to shake furiously a plasma was wandering around
unless it was the smoke of so many national-brand fags
national fag packets & butts covered the floor
the rapporteur began to scream
but undaunted they carried on discussing
including those who never
ever had discussed & never will discuss
& I kept writing through all of the headaches
toothaches broken back
such was the tiredness that my cock had got rope-thick
my balls felt as if about to burst
I kept writing I was scared that if I stopped
the world's engine would stop
it seems god has created the world
& I've got to keep it going
each & everyone must give it a push forward
or everything will shamelessly collapse

17

the hammer blow
dead-on splitting the brick
the splinter the blow or the dazed splitting clear verse
to look at this thing as we lie dying or blinded
by the sudden flash of the blowtorch
or the guy who fell into the trench full of quicklime
the trench done & dug the baked stones offloaded
then with the water everything boiling & steaming
the boiling of the baked stones was the last thing he saw
iron god, plastic idols, the screw's hexagonal head,
the wafer had turned into a plastic disc,
the tin disc of veramon tablets,
capsules, priming capsule, space capsule,
gold or other metal leaf encapsulating the teeth,
metal sheath containing explosive,
the hammer blow splitting the explosive capsule,
priming capsule,
the tin box of veramon tablets

18

in the game of three cards you get shafted
because you feel smart (the winning card is always the other one)
lucky the elections have come & gone
I've had it with walking around
posting hammers & sickles everywhere
I still prefer swimming in the river
feeling water as it slides over me
hearing frogs as they sing their throats dry
singing fishes loud amphibious songful fishes
I can still see in front of me
the guy who could catch fish with his hands
there can't be too many people
who can catch live fish with their hands
in triumph he shows us the swish of his coveted catch
my father will be a frog fisher into extreme old age
& here I am repeating to myself the platonic poem on the frog
that songful voice auspicious in the final hour
leaping with its voltaic legs between mud & mud
they pare their life down to zero to survive the winter frosts
to wake from near-death with each spring
to work the fun fairs work the dodgems
to leap from car to car
like the frog leaps from mud to mud
afterwards I'd see a night-time Rimini
the houses like mushrooms sprung up overnight

we survive by transforming ourselves into all the animals of creation
the Friulian guy wanted to talk into the last hours of the night
the wooden walls were dripping water that shook with the passing trains
the days were passing through me & I through them like nothing's the
    matter
auspicious songs in the final hour
we'd speak words of love to each other as the girl
stabbed the knife quickly between the splayed fingers
we'll be able to eat flames fly into hoops of fire
auspicious songs in the final hour

For My Daughter

you'll have to brave water fire darkness
you'll have to stay human despite the fine-spread brutalization
to touch all the elements of death unto death
live through all that has never been lived & never will be again
don't believe a word of all the words they'll say to you
we who also live to stand for all those who have died
as long as one is left standing defeat has not yet happened
as long as our pages endure
not the buried rose but our buried class
we're in the chaos before creation before the verb
let there be light & darkness came
let there be a man & a pig came
a Jew in Nazi Germany
a Palestinian in Israel
a Black in South Africa
not the buried rose but the disappeared
the massacred buried communists
our buried soul
we who stand for
all of those who were
& all of those who will be

25

perhaps one day my son will tell my grandson
that granddad was a communist & this phrase
will take on an absurd flavour
as if you'd been told my granddad
was a Jacobin & regicide
anyway I've done nothing but write verse
I've put paper in front of the beast
& when I wrote a long poem for a birthing
that had suddenly happened in the Vicolo Borgia
a long poem of which only one verse remains
'your feet that have not yet touched the earth'
—this is a verse you'll be able to use
for a deity not yet incarnated
despite everything incarnated as I was

on the shop floor where I work they'd burn powder detergent
to lubricate the wires being driven through the draw bench
this universe would be more bearable
if it didn't have the stench of cremation ovens
the stench of the devoured of Sabra & Shatila
the green flies laying eggs on the eyes of the massacred
flies clustered in their wide-open eyes
laying new flies in honour of the lord of the flies

My Son Adrian

it's precisely by Adrian's daddy being turned
inside out on all sides that the totality can be expressed
what matters is not to be enlightened or benighted
but for any changes to be swift & painless
the most metaphysical absurdity is that certain feral beasts
make Stalin & Molotov seem nice
it is in the clash of feral beasts
that the world's supreme balance is maintained
& how is it possible to change the world & keep sewers working
& road systems electric power plants most intricate telephone networks
it's wanting to change the world without changing a thing
revolutions are made precisely
in a final attempt to save the indispensable
stave off all that's useless so as to save our vitality
someone said that it was with the restoration
that the spirit of the French revolution conquered the world
it's like saying that imbecility is precisely what makes the world go round
I've seen certain flowers spring up in the cracks of frost
grass is grass anywhere but when it makes it through
a small crack in the tarmac it amazes us
we're sinners we're sentenced no use repeating that
we need the opposite homily: we're holy & saved
the threeternal father (sic) must have got it into his head
to keep the human species going for an eternity
if it's true that Eskimo women get pregnant
even at seventy degrees below zero

33

the common grave is the resting place of my class
we've no identity a collective mass—to disappear leaving no trace
to return to the womb of nature most fertile as she is
& here come the pretty graves the most idiotic angels
the so-called high arts of the rich
a very ceremonious beauty flamboyant as it is
the game of pretty statues with the most ceremonious pretty faces
the bishops in their white mitres sacredy-polished with holy oil
well fed & placid by effective grace & divine providence
—to make all this desperation into our joy
with much gentleness all of this will disappear
writing without ceremony requires uncommon intelligence
the end of the model can be symbolized
by the upending of all values
weaving new beginnings by this language
requires the tenderness of human drives to flourish in flight over
    the paper
only by hallucination will you be able to see in what I write
the heartbeat of new events

34

there's a precise correlation between the clamour of rhetorical figures
& the level of beastliness
I head for the factory I put up with
all the ridicule from the still-sleeping world
overcoming the horror of the model requires
a fearsome resistance to suffering
a realism pared down to pure speculation
an entirely improbable realism
there's more than enough reality & I have to live through it all
to write Aesopisms or dada
it is in pure casualness that the thing is expressed
each sign has turned into a dragon

armed with the episcopal letter I turned up at the factory gate to be
     hired
'please shelter this soul plunged into despair by the idleness of
     unemployment'
perennial is change & nothing's perennial but this
when Adrian was born the galaxies shivered
the planets were all sheer above him
a whirlwind lifted the last barn full of freshly mown hay
then the time will come of binary systems of decimations & pocket
     parakeets
the problems of silica transistors royal card games
living in a less desperate way requires everything be inscribed
& if you want to write poems you'll have to know the gods' awful fate
if you want to be a steelworker you'll need extreme speed & extreme
     rigour
Indians or Africans South Americans Asians
I'm prole deluxe by comparison
the Palestinian is perfect without a homeland left casting the last
     stone
& this little red-headed parakeet is also perfect
with his rainbow tail busy as he is desperately defending his cage
the crimes get more & more frightening
because we live in a frightening system
that not even the bosses can stand without their daily cocaine
the factory that'll survive is the one that'll best organize the order of
     destruction

so as to improve your endurance
you'll need to imagine yourself as long dead
suspended between life & death
the world will be seen in the most sublime transparence
& it's not true that everyone was fascist under fascism
many were simply nothing at all for nearly all of the 24 hours in a day
& it's because of all this nothing
that poetry must lash out in heavy stanzas with no jumps
to end a poem by the lack thereof
the last page a death certificate
& let that at least not be repetitive

39

such was my poverty & powerlessness
I seized the language & with my face over the abyss
like a madman I dominated a language universe
the muse starry as she was
got spellbound watching all those lunar craters
the monkey's swagger was insatiable
& I managed to be pissed off & happy
as I waited to be rewarded by the enemy
we'll always end up somewhere south of some bright idiot
the relentless call of freshness of intuition
the thing is not absolutely eternal
not bad that I've at least caught a glimpse of it
the miracle has come to pass & will not be repeated
the reader is lucky it can all be read in a few hours
it took me ten years to find it
& I wrote without the least awareness
of my own limits including the orthopaedic ones
quick as I was to leap at nothingness

40

martyred by lapsus by repetition
the whole will come across as a variation on the same anguish
for forty years Italian has not been my daily language
the reader is far off almost defunct
an intolerable burning on the open wound
& me day in day out terrorized
by the fear of being torn apart by dogs
—to hide the author to make him incognito
to not take part to deny yourself hide live leaving no trace
to dissociate yourself to disappear
as a poet I was a pure non-existence
yet I persisted enjoying the usual orgasms
& no one can imagine
where all those little balloons will end up
that float in our air

Apprenticeships
(1978)

I

a clock set to the split microsecond stamps the attendance card
& in attendance I start up all the starter motors
god has to move perennially in perennity the prime of all movers
satan in the centre of the unmoving his ass wedged in saved from the
    nausea
I clock in on the world's evolved skins my tongue hitting the few sound
    teeth I've got left
—to finish & start again until total nausea to hit away at the nail head
not to upend the umbrella the cup no matter what happens
to accept everything with the whole coffin box & be resurrected
    between sheets of corrugated cardboard
to hold the box aloft that boxes the fragile universes in
all must be boxed taken in & swathed there's a danger of general
    breakdown
the call stuns you dazes you—to be in the thick of calls is the condition
at each gate a new one until the last deep plunge
dazed by the colourful scraps of glass & shot at
in the toilets drawings of women with huge gashes ready for the
    swallowing
into the softest membrane & he falls out into the social organism
to clock in & out & the toil begins again of having to breathe I'll end
    up wheelground
anything I touch seems important to me I cleave to it & so they don't
    wheelgrind me
by metalizing & fossilizing myself I will become completely inedible

man can be measured by his time signature mine is fast & hits you
    head on
—to try for the final opening to stride over into the limitless up to the
    ultimate nausea
even a pebble thrown into water was enough to start up the nausea
in these faster & faster spots of the world to start over up to the
    ultimate nausea
in this hell to accept the part of devil to run even faster
in the end a totally suitable man will be selected salvation is not an
    option

III

they try to stop him being born & he bursts through the rubbers takes
　　advantage of forgetfulness
& strides over & reaches not becoming or transformations but simply
　　birth
in the womb he turns upside down encased in the chain mail that locks
　　him in
—to attack even when you risk being crushed
it's not possible to refuse if I can't see death in what I refuse
if I can't see in each beginning the beginning of all beginnings
the unfailing hunger that can't be sated knowledge begins with its pangs
I stick my finger in your mouth to take out the object that'd choke you
—to stride over for a universe chewed by your precious teeth
to shake somnolence fill the lungs with air use the mouth
all of it in the objects you chew I grow inside you fantastic you outside
　　of hell
—to stride over for a universe chewed by your precious teeth
to baptize caterina they are blowing on the resounding teeth of the organ
he bends to find the page it's been a week since christ has risen all in gold
chalices are raised & lowered blessings blast out loud
eat of these loaves those who do won't ever again feel the pangs of
　　hunger
the best of my sperm cells strode over monsters with their open mouths
& swooped on the egg wedged in with its head sucking away

X

the machine is moving but many pieces of the machine are mutually still
a cat when it moves moves every part of the cat also relative to
     everything
I am in movement but the verses will stay fixed until they move them
—to write verse like a corpse breeds writhing worms
a preferably new word close-up verses preferably antagonistic
many keys have sprung but only one letter has swooped on the page
anything that falls you bounce it back onto the keyboard
including user instructions
user distortions user distractions & user destructions
each word has the importance it deserves
& if I can't find what I'm looking for I'll find all the rest to make up
     for it
the most impressive tale is that of the tortoise
who couldn't be reached while all the rest could
the clock hand gains space visible & noiseless it spins on the
     living hours
my position is not neutral in this position they might well
     wheelgrind me
mars may be inhabited by some unicellular organisms
if someone can have one fixed idea we've got many cells
& some kill themselves unable to live on this well-oxygenated earth
if there's the joy of existing there's also the strain of existing
—to approach everything & sure enough everything concerns me in a
     carnal way

the first reading is hard
but if you can read it once you'll read it a third time even
my dreams have no spoken languages
I can only dream them when awake & I write them down directly

XII

poems must be read one at a time & in silence
I don't think but write directly hit it out in Italian
& get hit with all the rest
my teacher taught me to write by hitting the rod on my fingers
since content was dropped on me & hit me
I'll write it out hit it out
in vietnam they even use wasps against the americans
you can use books too in this case slam them in their faces
take one non-submissive word
an otherwise word suspended as long as there remains
a point of non-possible arrival where they tend to arrive
a shooting range that'll have you hit anything except that target
the empty sky—to get to fill it
when anguish is at its darkest
a quick flash a crack in the dark
& the dilated pupil not narrowing in that lightning glimmer
—to end so as to
start anew seesawing between hope & no hope
—to fall into it & come up again your pupil hugely dilated
& your pupil caterina dilated also from love
—to touch the walls of this house & may a wall open
& in continuous discovery into the universe where they couldn't come
& you're the first to come so the universe is caterinized
with the right aperture of the pupil

XIV

at times in that riot of machineries I get drowsy & fall asleep
—to fall into hibernation deep as possible & wake up loosened
at times I don't want to sleep cos if I sleep they'll come & get me
I used to run away & they wouldn't come for me
now they come for me & I can't run
& surely sleeping is no better than staying awake
being a man I must pass through & they don't always let me
you always die & are not always born
it should be a language you can only use in writing
rather get busy use yourself up than get used
let's try to break certain orders but without too many falls
I'll go & touch my wife
if I get you pregnant there's no danger of anyone else doing it
with desperate joy since I am in perpetual movement
& unaware of my position in the chain
—to find something to break & if I work deep I'll type holes into the paper
the beauty of the system is that you can imagine you're outside it
—to hide in the paper & if I work deep I'll plunge deep into the depth
—to write imagining a sky that closes but can also open
—to get serious about verb creation being not a thing but an entering into
if you go to the cinema it's not bad what's worse is having to pay on the
    way out as well
in the belly of capitalism in the belly of the beast
(the only hope is the end)
in this precise instant I'm living through there are only the pieces
(I only remember what I used to love)

in this precise suspended instant
(I remember what I used to hope for)
to count all the steps in one day to keep careful count
the acid-disfigured woman could recognize herself best by not looking
    in the mirror
peter heard the cock crow three times & didn't get wheelground
if it's a collapsing world we should have a collapse festival
between all the opposites & also stay normal
—to dilate one word until it can contain all words
I might stop seesawing but the seesawing will surely not stop
if god doesn't exist I'm stuck with continuing to exist
in those milky days lived through & travelled through & that travelled
    through me
the statues with their swelling paps will give liquid plaster milk
you'll be able to throw yourself into the same writing any number
    of times
your joy clotting up to the last bursts
the higher the brightness the darker the sense
to hit on tooth decay until the bone cracks
the scream that'll have your denture jump out of your mouth
the unleashed ultimate anguish at the hardened chaos
the exit from the bellies from the floods still stained with death
nailed to the four limbs & us un-nailed & crucified

XVII

to hit away at this typewriter until you drive them mad hitting writing
delving into a poem means you want to write holes into the paper
discard wishful thinking do away with the hole in the paper too
no regrets the only dignity is to be outside & against
here's the stone—to scatter seed on it when even stones sprout
    green shoots
everything bred astonishments gleamings
charged up as I was into worlds of ultimate optimism & lucidity
hitting the wedge until the wee critter zips out
glass metals plastics I lift an arm lift a leg
but while I write I can only write I'm trying all sorts
the fingers swoop on the keys too much agitation in following
    inspiration
the wee levers of my olivetti lettera 22 get tangled up
—to write on such paper & repeat everything to myself as I shave
putting my face on to go out into these streets
one production done I start the next I the underwritten & overwritten
    yourstruly
with mostly lost faiths there's one ultimate faith
in something empty & vegetal the faith that I cannot die wheelground
seesawing between two opposite faiths & skipping over both
I'm certain I exist even though the proofs are void & if I get precise
    I'll disappear
to be a survivor you need to have existed before & also after
void faith in my wife's existence I get in touch with that & she gets
    pregnant

—to search for the invention that by chance hits on a real character
that by change hits on my own self
there's no centre each blow hits me head on
I'm upended I won't straighten up

XIX

I've done nothing but weld wires six millimetres across
I don't even know what the use will be of these lines of verse that grow
    longer & longer
if writing is a condition it's not precisely my condition
it's not about knowing the ending it's about not falling too much
& also hitting centres on centres laying the priming wires on the holes
& under the beds ready to lay bombs
into the mouths of the sleeping Americans
not even in the ravings of dreamtime measles
during the red rashes inside a bomb-raided skin
they come light they do really light
you who are wife & ark who carry laughing mortals
& swell up until the final pop the emptying out
a new mortal is passing through laughing amid the horrors
all told it's us in cellular scatterings & we sleep peaceful nights
we who sleep each night & get up falling deep

XXII

he comes out of the vagina plummets out head first
in the image of the first one plummeting out & redeemed by the
    magnificent cross
the revolution because we're extremely happy with hope in an
    abstract faith
cardiac & respiratory rhythm rhythm of the several plummeting
    alphabet letters
from that sand he touched the sea with his pretty toes
I shave once a week can't say I'm ashamed of my beard now
I saw a last supper only judas was dark christ was the blondest &
    bluest of the lot
oppressed & mostly depressed & it's not like I'm open more like
    they're coming to open me
& so open I was swallowing the divine wafer the crucified victim
they kill them even though it costs more to kill them than to
    feed them
& the trophies of heaps of shoes
(with very round stones we smashed the last glass panes
knocked on the knockers of the last doors
the gutted werewolves turned into massive stenches
the bomb raids were followed by great silences
we were trying to smash the final silence)

XXV

cats stuffed full of fish heads
the heads crunched by the thin teeth needles more like
christ has drunk & eaten & not only because thy kingdom's coming
john sat next to christ to get the best morsel
christ is setting a meal today & those who partake will never again
    feel the pangs of hunger
to be sated for ever no more working away with your teeth
& tenderly sated to lay your head on christ's chest
to decode the world even as the censer clouds the altar
& for an instant it will be perfumed shadows or souls
give us our bread give us our exact wine
it might be true that the downtrodden will be the new rulers
but changing saves me from the boredom
of seeing the same old prides on the same old men
—to sand off the pride petrified on that face
today is the day for the harvest for us to sweat in that ripe elation

XXVIII

as you went off with the marks of crucifixion intact
swallowed into a huge skyblue inhumed in that skyblue
escaping the dissecting knife the bone forceps
the rounded hooks the arched saw
nostalgia for you grew huge as you disappeared upwards
(by dissecting the corpses of the starved we succour life)
escaping maceration of the bones scarification
desiccation of the guts
you were gravitating closer & closer to the spirit & the father
happier & happier as you faded away
you'll see the suspended earth our sunset our resurrection
the corpses for dissection get rarer & rarer
they could have used the mad people in madhouses
the old in the asylums so poor precious & consumptive
all of those who were burst apart by existence
would be met by the scalpels the mercury syringe
maceration in the tub the fridge's mouth
you outside the planets with the dippers & dwarves contracted
    after the last throb
bursting the last border to the last skin
escape velocity rising to crack all the walls burst out of all walls
your eye still full of skyblue earth
(the eye is taken from the socket by excision etc)
with your earthly eye still full of skyblue earth
(the sharpest scalpel in that eye)

after a catastrophe of years in an endless vertigo the last error touched
on a calm day or a calm night where a kingdom is still possible
with a last hope brushing against all deaths all fears
in this earth that plummeted down as you rose

XXXI

dead capital having to be resurrected by sucking live blood
the cancer factory will live the longer the more it sucks & as it sucks it
    doles out cancers incarnate
death has me by the throat I have death in my throat (bruno barilli)
in the factory surgery open wide the lead fillings & bits of denture
    examined
scraper on the decay nerves touched bloodied spit in the automatic
    spittoon
chloroform water the forceps tearing you open pull hard a bunch of
    blood in your mouth
rubber hammer hits your knee how nicely the leg jerks
to read all the letters of the graduated table first one eye then with all
    of your eyes
carefully examined palate throat tongue balls taps on the back
say the age of christ the great supremo of masonic lodges
you'll be hit by a proper number black spit in the pocket spittoon
the eye sockets are free of charge as the eye gets inflamed & blood-
    squirted
selected into a fright of stories the bubonic plagues the massacres &
    syphilises
all will revert to ash save for your polished glass eye
after the liberation those cancer-incarnate factories were also liberated
when they hanged mussolini the hierarchs & the one with her black
    stockings to the hooks
impregnating amid all the frights one rushing run after another

mice rats & voles would get onto the shop floor & their legs
    would give out
death capital needing to raise from the dead by holding death in
    its fist
death has me in its fist
a shop floor that stank like a buchenwald oven
at that place of burning anguish chewing on fear
in that catastrophe
those clenched fists of protest with death in our fists
death has you in its fist
here comes the drop of mercury the arsenic ddt arrow through a
    white-hot sky
arrow shot through an even brighter skyblue into the pure
nearer & nearer the poles the pure colds pure waters
the beating of your wings the heart beating inside you
the excitable speed of that heartbeat
save yourself save our souls

XXXIX

parish of santa caterina neighbourhood of santa caterina
communist section of santa caterina
inevitably my daughter should be called caterina the cat
they'd give us wafer offcuts & we'd consecrate bits of circumference
we buy the pharma wafer
the tablet so let's buy it what matters is the emptiness the face of
    the abyss
at the hospital I didn't die but saw men flow plummet finish
before the typewriter before the letters archetypes of all things
after a group of letters the rest came automatic
(out of the tomb all-night party with this suit & this starry necktie
I the underwritten yourstruly say I've not come from the all-nighter
    but from my own wake
while bombs are bursting & tearing you're going to the all-nighter
    with your necktie on
I'm going to cut your necktie off & you better grow some hair on
    your head
they cut my nails & beard then washed & stopped up all the holes)
at the moment when the lance passes the whole line
(I only exist when I write) in the registry ledgers the born & the
    dead marked down
an enormity of air breathers
(the future is what has not yet fallen on me)
if you manage the first verse then you'll write it all out
life for every hardwired life

when I stopped communion I started communicating & didn't get
    wheelground
—to write from the most remote place so as to be nearest
on this zero over this zero sat on this zero
& overcome I rise from this zero & from this zero write

XLI

& so I clearly saw the sties for the pigs with chewed-up ears
they slip & smash & shove & bite into each other for the swill a
    desperate grunting
to get fatter & fatter become meals & end up in ground-up chunks
I was rapporteuring with such sense of consequence
that everything became vague empty ready to vanish
there must be something whose trace remains when its memory is lost
a submerged memory
that trace that clue sought by sherlock holmes
who's stopped searching for whodunnit
but looks instead for the only place where it couldnaebeendun
pock-marked bomb-raided moon put a quarter moon in the
    monstrance
in the glowing of a flame in that ray of light piercing through
—to drink water from a spout held fast in the teeth of a pig-iron lion
on that last day on that square where everyone was exposed
only your earrings gleamed incarnate

XLIV

a snail once it's pulled its horns in will shut itself inside its own spittle
if it rains likely it'll be tied into a sack & made to ooze
it'll be cooked with a lot of sweet-smelling herbs & will send out its
    cooked horns
if I went back home I would perhaps find the last blue flax field
the sweetvetch blazing across the field was spreading into the roads
because of the progress of a madonna of the birth guarding a sacred foetus
    for eternity
& on we go with the mater & virgo & mystic rose & morning star
the tower of david the cross of all delights beyond the world's end
& you'll take pleasure in walking on the soft sweetvetch beyond the crack
    between houses
—to touch the high-power wires the shadow was touched by our tension
I could see the vibrations of the silver swords pronged into the sacred paps
those twilight vibrations in the seesaw of shadows
with a body dilated to include all bodies
—to strike a rapid flight (the taut elastic bands vibrating)
to hold the stricken prey frog or finch next to your heart
the red thistle flower that last throb inside of me
seesawing on the elastic branches for the leap to the highest branch
that childhood happy because the grown-ups were busy killing one
    another in filthy wars
again I can see the happiness of those grasses that rain
beating happily on the corrugated iron I could hear all the drops beating
the rain water draining out of the many iron waves
I could taste the rain's sharp flavour

smell the rain falling on the new bricks the dried earths
then of a sudden green leaves green grasses easy & calm again
not a breath of wind any more the wheat a well-rested sea
I must be feeling it as it grows the rain's made it even greener
the ear of wheat hardened the seeds happy (for all the red new dawns)

XLVI

your biggest thrill must have been pissing on your father's shoes
he kept your virginity hostage you were meant to save it for a
    sacramental love
on an iron bed in the chamber with several mirrors & sideboards full
    of neckties
where a white frigidity would be nothing but a hole made to bleed
a firecracker roams the kingdoms of cuckoldry & then turns into a
    mystical father a sacristy god
each operation stop-watched I split-second everything (so much fuss
    over poppycock)
eight hours sweated split-second-stop-watched (you beat competition
    with stop watches)
whoever gets on top of the maypole is a superman & can piss from
    that height
speaking of white frigidity & the maypole winner remember
franco fortini's white summits of the world for other eyeballs to come
(the rapist rapes the victim after throttling her with his necktie)
we're the champions of all things a stone splits a helmet & all the
    bright buttons
biking around the shop floor it's stuck & under threat the price of
    steel in freefall
brushing against all danger with the sickness stuck in the system
an original sin against which no baptism water has a snowball's chance
I'd get a postcard with the scent of your favourite palmolive soap
you'd mail inside a post bag (post horn) the smell of your nipples &
    thighs

anyway this story of the firecracker joyce also thought of that

see nausicaa chapter thirteen then the nationalist cyclops came

or nazzzzzzzzionalista with a thousand zeds as the fascist teacher would
pronounce it

& hit my fingers if I didn't write it down exactly the way he couldn't
pronounce it

the favourite scent was also on the more sensitive nipple

so as to spill into the orgasm pleasures (no it's not just a bleeding hole
you blockhead)

we'd watch certain faces that are always everywhere

you were the rare extra in a film the only one who

breaks the boredom of seeing the same face more or less disguised

we'd climb the tower staircase & ah suddenly to get to the Picene
brightness the light

all the square & rectangular fields all the possible imaginable browns
& greens

I could find you incarnated in all the walls in all the verses of the
Loreto litany

carrying all our joy on our backs until the release

of all the fishes in the aquariums all the birds in the cages

in a relentless guerrilla a relentless release

L

there was a time when I wrote
more than I would read
when I screamed more than I would listen
instead of seeing what was on TV there was an instant when I was
    seen by all
in genoa laid out & massacred by state police
you must keep silence even though they're mangling your balls
(do not name a shameful name)
you must say no for all eternity
after thirty years of privilege & corruption it's enough to have eight
    signatures
as if eight signatures in a row were enough
billions of blood signatures won't be enough
let us imagine all iron knots
all entanglements simply loosened
if you can't loosen it all then cut do something react
look it's coming for you do something get out of the way by god
it's ready to swallow you save yourself!

LIII

all water ice all snow all water
a man is pretty much made of rainwater that has rained & is raining
with all this rainwater I carry on me
all the water of lakes all the lakes
water rivers water sea water stream
water of rain & womb water flowing underneath
slick helmets of hair-cream that dripped melting away in the warm
    rays of the sun
they're biting away at a gleaming heap of corpses
holed bodies are leaking water deflated perforated
fine then perforate away since everything's in a heap
you need to write about a precise subject
& have everything turn around fast
stalin a general secretary
O fair stars of the Bear the servants' quiet work
then nothing was quiet neither the works nor luckily the servants
in the Firman firmament & under a great attack of full & empty
a huge fear suspended in that Firman firmament
dripping away replacing it drained away—to recognize—to be with
    these verbs

Repression: A User Manual

(1980)

LIV

it might happen that you have to wear a cassock over the fascist uniform
with my double cassocks I was seesawing the censer raising perfumed puffs
to the one who is in the all to the one who would burst without being burst
within all anguishes he the one with no anguish
if the time of creation is nothing to him
for us it is an eternity with no way out ever
so I was still mud when I snapped thermometers
to feel the drop of mercury on my hand
the drop of iron will pierce the hand through
the mercurial pollutions are the most dangerous save yourself from the drop
hide your human stench if you don't want the dog to find & strangle you
if you put your brain in the exploiters' service it will burn out on the spot
everything was dead rapid the letters were flying from under me
forgive the reckless joy that has leapt on me
& we who are immortal at the service of new men
I can assure you that new men need no one's services
or user manuals for a more or less imaginary repression
that mouth leers hawks spits plagiarizes
I hawk spit parry feint leer

LVII

we were walking in that cemetery where ibsen has a beautiful stone on
    top of him
a graveyard full of bankers shipowners ice exporters
beautiful artists with most beautiful haloed grass
I think this lovely haloed grass should make my wife happy
instead she's yelling at me saying that on our Sunday walks
I always take her to the filthiest places
(heads turn to look at us
four pigeons flutter among the tombs)
the filthiest animals are the ones who live closest to man
(this is my wife's lyrical yelling
heads turn again to look at us)
in the end to make my wife laugh I point at the graves & say
'O rabid worms devour one another in peace'
& this time my wife starts laughing
but heads turn yet again to look at us
I think my wife is the last-comer
& finds herself in her homeland completely expatriated & estranged
& she could only have married a guy like me
who's completely expatriated & estranged from everything
as if this expatriation & estrangement were the only possible land
this present is the graveyard of our future
these people the undertakers of our future
(I turn round sharply to look at them)
they're nodding their heads you can't even tell if they exist
we've fallen into the filthiest place & maybe it doesn't even exist

LVIII

all right quickly wash all the floors in the world
pick up all they've tossed away all they've lost
with the broom that sweeps with the rag that scrubs the floors piecework
wash everything quickly with your wet rag hit them in the face
bleach & rag hit the world
with this denture I have wholly imaginary toothaches
you'll never lose your job as long as there's men many stinks
wash down the family house too
keep the kids in line check their furry tongues
the mother calls the kids by desperate names
buys the shirts the socks the underwear
you'll never manage to buy it all
since you were two months old you've known what to expect
all I ask is that you don't come in here & mess up my papers
I keep order at bay through an even more implacable hell
the writings should be equally dire
the beard was not shaven for the wee morning kiss
keep everything off burst out atrociously
I've hung up the metaphysical print of a piazza
my son points at the piazza with his tiny finger
& says that's where we were before we got born
we couldn't expect a society divided into classes

LIX

the rain beats on the tender grass in great thirst
put a grass blade between your lips & blow
it will vibrate between your lips it vibrates
pick a serrated grass blade no matter if it rains
in the endless multiplied rains
a big raindrop walking
upend your umbrella on the door
touch a horseshoe
—to see an unknown world see it anew
my grandfather would show me the liner that took him to argentina
a bunch of smoke chasing after you
he looked at us from under the rain with his best hat on as if he were
  about to be executed
or to start making love in his best hat
the new days & those to come were looking at one another in
  amazement
guard your seed inside a sweet sweet vagina
if she doesn't have a magnificent orgasm it's like tossing your sperm
  down the toilet
seems you can't toss yourself into the same orgasm twice
this alphabet dilates the schema into a stupefied provisional timescale
the cock was ptolemaic everything should revolve around its head
& she who's meant to take it into her hands & her mouth too
when she wouldn't want to take anything more into her hand or
  mouth
& in fact would gladly do without even looking at it

LX

smash the image gather up the pieces of image glue everything back
    up again
I read about all they can do to a man (they can do that too)
hell's fantasy has no extreme though it runs towards the extremes
christ imagined that if they drank divine blood they'd find drinking
    human blood disgusting
I could see the thing as if these eyes were another's
even the adversity of verse entirely vectorized
into this poetry that scratches & terrifies me
having in fact nothing to lose
I could write anything at all they can't very well chase me from the
    Norwegian factory
for writing mostly terror-driven Italian poems
don't mess yourself up with imaginary blood
imaginary blood drips from the cracks
with the alphabet you can chase after everything
they manage to fight fascism by all becoming fascists
I can write that too I only hope it doesn't exist
don't believe a single word from those who have power over us
you absolutely need to remember what day it is today
I must be absolutely normal in my behaviour
& never answer gospitblood when someone says good morning
writing poems is dead easy all you need is the courage to swallow
    everything
I'd got myself an infrared lens to watch the solar eclipse
the shadow was eating the luminous shield

the sun being released from the eclipse
does not at all mean we'll be released from our anguish
but as long as we can feel joy for anything that is released
it means our desperate struggle is not defeated
our joy is the ultimate sign

LXIV

I used to wash dishes in a tavern in Rome
where totally down-at-heel poets from Rome would come to eat
spit in the dishes it's fun someone said
poets came with no bellies no stubble cheeks scraped & shaven
we'd manage to spit up the magnificent soups with greasy gobs
I soon got tired of seasoning soups with magnificent gobs
eye no see heart no hurt but I went to see it all
so I go to milan & find work as a ringer of doorbells
ringing doorbells I was trying to sell associated publishers' books by
    instalments
how salt is the taste of this repeated ringing of others' doorbells
on that occasion I met fortini I'd rung his doorbell too
he read a few of my poems & so fortini discovered there was no timeline
I humbly confess I don't get it yet
he read me one of his poems too about a piece of dry wood
a facile allegory not that I managed to understand it as usual
luckily afterwards (perhaps to clear both of our palates) he read to me
a poem by rimbaud on biblical hungers
—to eat split stones pebbles scattered by the floods
a poem I found perfectly suited to my situation
for a month I rang all the doorbells
& all I managed to sell was the first volume of mao's collected works
maybe that lone buyer became a terrorist
there was this big splash the theory of the hundred flowers to blossom in
    one vase
Togliatti was so charmed by the hundred flowers

133

that he was sorry he hadn't learnt chinese
so destalinization breaks out very well let's destalinize
I hadn't clocked that destalinization would be done by going
     rightwing
by the virgin mary I swear I hadn't got it
so I rush over to see a clandestine Bordigan friend where I always went
when I couldn't crack a mystery
Bordiga said the catastrophic crisis won't happen for another 20 years
(here I am waiting) meanwhile let's have fun selling a book a month
let's ring all the doorbells & in the end I'll fail to feed
even the crabs clinging to my balls
I was scratching desperately

LXVII

I've written about the last supper or party meeting at the outer-
　　most borders
I've written about my father & the ants (an anthole in the mouth)
my wife too had an ant father but hers was a much worse asshole
　　than mine
my father told me if I manage to eat
one raw lemon a day I'll survive anything
my wife told her father she was in love with an Italian communist
don't mind if he's a communist but Italian that's the pits
let's hope to survive with these poems
& maybe not have to eat whole raw lemons
the disproportion between what I see
& what I manage to write rises & plummets
that street full of scattered primary-school books covered in blood
they make roads with no pavements the better to wheelgrind
　　people
there must be some hidden plot in everything
now the historic town centre is rife with packs of dogs
their mottled fur full of worms
I was holding the goose down & chopped its head off with the
　　hatchet
& the terrorized headless goose shot off down the slope
I was running after it the structural substance of the story remains
　　unchanged
my father with a huge wound
I took photos of them standing by a wall with death on their faces

they looked like people about to be executed
the bride & groom particularly funereal
to make babies & properly socialize them by dint of slaps &
    smacks
don't tell lies in front of the bosses don't take the stuff of bosses
let them take everything your sweat & piss & spunk
if you've whupped up much frustration
you're married now you can slap her around scot-free
if she's whupped up much frustration she can lay into the kids
the kids will run & look for others particularly harmless others
those who have nothing better will hang lizards & cats wreck
    birds' nests
and on with the correspondence of loving senses
if they're wheelgrinding their dentures let's smash those teeth up

LXVIII

on a day that is all spitting blood & toil
eight hours that end well after we're crushed & broken
on a day when even the bright sunlight
is particularly pukey
we were looking into each other's eyes bloodshot with the same dust
& you suddenly said to me
that christ had a twin brother satan
& immediately all the heresies of the oppressed are in front of my eyes
all of them flashing in front of me christ might also not have been dead at all
& be living somewhere guarding the book of the ultimate magic
the secret formulae by which we would be able to do anything
& that virgin's belly cheerfully guarding an eternal & desperate struggle
you kept telling me that everybody knew those things very well
these are things everybody knows & no one will have the courage to talk about
only the likes of us can tell each other side by side on the same machine
the same exact despair
the same sweat

LXIX

we had the first one leaning against the parliament house portal
& as it happened she had a beautiful orgasm & got pregnant as well
quick loves filling life with glamour
the outbreak of the most beautiful love in all the parliamentary
    histories of the world
& we also had news of the murky black scheming from the sacred
    family
& social services planning the most revolting abortion in the world
not clear if they wanted the abortion because the nordic aryan
    germanic girl
was impregnated by a dago
or because the impregnation
happened almost inside the most beautiful parliament house in
    the world
we decided we'd tuck into it all the fuckings the children
the delivery happened without pains or sweats
ourselves being preadamitic that is not subjected
to the sin of the apple theft by adam & beautiful eve
we celebrate the happiest event in all parliamentary histories
we imagine all those who'll be born happily for joy
I got into the hospital full of women lying there as if gutted
    deathly pale
mary in a rage ready to jump up wash up dirty up smash up
scrape off all the dirt with the purest acids & bleach
we'll wash & dirty everything together I laugh you laugh he laughs
to love each other between sheets smelling of air earth & sunlight

a dirty fog will also come down stick everything back in the washing
    machine
I laugh you laugh he laughs
someone gets pissed off if I laugh if you laugh if today tomorrow
    we laugh

LXX

yesterday the crane-lift crashed down in one
everyone disappeared behind that massive dust cloud
a sudden crack of materials it cracked
in the dead of night the thud I saw the driver jump off & save himself
before the great dust rose I saw that jump
the acrobat found a line stretched at the right place dead right
a spark from electric wires touching ran all along the line all across the
    shop floor
the great valve will blow up wait for the great valve to blow up
the foreman took out a book
where all the great crashes are meant to be preemptively listed
a handful of sawdust is enough to block everything
(you can't foresee everything)
if a handful of sawdust is enough to block everything
you need total consensus
night-time phonecalls begin
wake up all the maintenance foremen
the maintenance underforemen & maintenance repairmen
they come running with blowtorches all around the beast
around the crash
they ran here & there all around the corpse
checked the timers
measured the screws snapped clean off suddenly snapped off
(an air bubble)
when panic strikes every man runs helter-skelter

a handful of sawdust is enough to block everything
an oil stain the banana peel
the driver saved himself the joy of seeing him happily hanging up there
below him he could see the crash the multiplied sparks flying in the dusts
the blowtorch was throwing huge fitful shadows around the shop floor
so should the system crash with us happy & safe hanging off wires
in a great dust in a sea of sparks will-o'-the-wisps festive fireflies
of a gloomy night luminous semblances seeds of a happy day

LXXI

lock up a real pig on the shop floor

not a normal pig

a pig I mean a hog I mean lock him up on the shop floor eight hours
 solid

let's see how the society for the protection of animals will react

let's see how the pig will react to this extreme cruelty

he'll blow burst choke get mad & possessed by demons let's see if he's
 still edible

let's see if his nervous system has broken down or not

let's see if he's become impotent his sex whittled & twisted like a
 corkscrew

if he's survived & not burst apart let's free the pig

let's take him to the many abandoned lands

put him out to pasture & let him dig up roots & highly prized truffle

you've survived a terrible breakdown now enjoy

kick around in freedom breathe pure airs get your fill

yet this indicative proposal cannot be accepted

the pig has been selected so he will fatten tender pork chops

extra thin ham slices

& fatten an extrafat brain

for the disgusting pork saveloys get your fill get fat get rested

you're lined up for a long knife

those who work on the shop floor were selected for something entirely
 different

hold out through a whole season against the breakdown

you're a different animal no use chopping you up

you've got to hold out in one piece
(you'll be further & further selected till you burst)
stick a man on the shop floor
lock them in eight hours solid
see how he reacts
take a man of humanism take him away
from the pictures the frescoes of great humanists
take this most humanized man see how he'll react
test it many times over let's see what happens
see if he gets dangerous
(he might get dangerous
those who work in a factory for endless hours solid
can get very dangerous
bug all the telephones
prise his brain open see what ideas he's brewing
measure his rage
expect it to burst)

LXXII

once me & mary were dreaming we were fucking
& gently as we woke up from that dream
gently realized
that as well as dreaming of fucking we were in fact fucking
& we touched the top of our being the glorious magic
you read about that devil invading bolshevik russia
it wreaks much havoc bolshevik countries are left with no trace of
    holy water
we can bathe in holy water
I scream into her ears bosses of the world go eat one another
& that idiot starts laughing
even through a piece of denture missing
& you muse or cunt sing the supreme pissed-off state the supreme joy
sing to me of your dear gifts for all the red new dawns
everything can be revved up to dizzy speeds
we were torn apart only starved of collective life
as we woke from this delirium

LXXIX

on this day the snow is gusting down almost horizontally
it's whitewashing all the walls facing that direction on that day
the north-facing branches fill with heavy & very wet snow
the snow races past it's almost horizontal the gusts bending it
the west–east running train will be all snowed up on one side
the drips on the glass panes draw increasingly horizontal commas even
    higher up
by measuring the slant of drips the snow's slant
you'll measure the speed of that entirely imaginary train
inside the train you'll never know if you're motionless or spinning at
    dizzy speed
often you won't know a thing even if you look out the window
there should be a guy outside standing stock-still & looking at me
    looking at you all
if I too walk east–west I'll be all snowed up on one side
on this easter friday with its overcast overhang
the scattergun bursts from this typewriter
on this day I feel as if I'm looking down eternal snow-white time
one time flows past as magnificent alphabet letters click & shoot out
the crisis is such that they can no longer foul up the snow
I imagine I'm looking down a white eternity waiting to be written
the survivors of Hitler's massacres
immediately rushed to massacre the Palestinians
this aquarium fill it with spit
I dreamt of swarms of fishes

roaming through clear bright airs
(O severe mathematics
your clear bright air)

LXXX

the poems are getting longer & longer—shorten them at dizzy speed
the more I try to dizzily shorten them the longer they dangerously grow
in st peter they swallowed the wafer with maximum indifference
it seems the only one who still believes is me a follower of davide lazzaretti
killed with a pistol shot by a carabiniere
if you want my blood come & get it & they did right away
dear red brigades you better give over
if you're the avengers you'll never manage to avenge us all
I feel like I'm being studied
he does everything calmly but ten yards off
I deny everything the information I've written is totally fabricated
I certainly deserve a harsh sentence
after moro's kidnapping I thought they'd look for the logistic base of
    terrorism
inside my typewriter
I felt guilty for your sins all of you
now let's not make too much of this
everything will fall into maximum indifference
being is nothingness that's why it's in perpetual motion
the only cure that works against my persecution mania
is hegel's doctrine of being
suicide as a magical act one kills oneself
& thinks he's destroyed a whole world
while it's this world that seeks our destruction

LXXXI

I've chosen to express maximum vitality through poems
I who learnt very late to read to speak to write
—overcome that hurdle for all eternity
what matters is how you manage to live with all these monsters
    getting called up
they throw them at me I ought to hang them on the wall
absolve all the evils in the world don't stay plunged in this muck
you who will all inherit the blank papers of a great tranquillity
in order to be very clear you must be in great danger
everything will turn to mush let's take advantage of it
buy a thousand fresh sheets & write them all up swiftly
& if a coup comes down sweep up all those sheets
beat them with sticks without breaking their bones they're still
    needed to weave
in the end there were so many weavers they could afford to cripple
    half of them
jail jehovah witnesses
who do nothing but further delay the end of this world
after publishing that poem I felt guilty
I see the whirlwind of these letters no matter what I print it's atrocious
I tell her the wife I mean that my poems
are about catties taking walkies on the roofs
—to write most revolting poems with no hope
they'll read well when there's no more hope
when I write certain letters it's like I'm writing to the non-existent
I can't understand poetry I can only write it
when it can be understood no one will waste time writing it

LXXXIV

I don't skull any more arsenic it makes me too drowsy
as long as I'm writing capital I've got to keep my brain sharp (marx)
they're so sweet with the fuck-may-care-ness of an entirely imaginary
    power
I was in a hotel with materials such as solidified fossil fuel (I was trapped)
go & see the librarian lady make love & borrow the magic books
the question of joy has got complicated
roversi writes that joy is not to be trusted
a few years earlier he wrote that anguish serves oppression
I'm quoting the poem of our derangement for you
all this joy see if you can manage to pull it along
poetry like a red-hot blade cutting through a bladder of lard
there are miraculous moments when verb & praxis are one
no use denying it you barbsqueak there are such moments
dangerous levels of DDT discovered in the milk of motherly breasts
which really shows sanguineti was right about the dirtiest mothers
& quasimodo wrong with his stuff about the sweetest mothers
still you must remember that when quasimodo's mother was breastfeeding
DDT didn't yet exist & so couldn't poison anyone
poetry is like a bolt out of the blue that suddenly uncovers
the filth we're forced to live through
a flash of light that leaves you dazed & unbelieving
there was a time when reading croce could give me the deepest sleeps
as long as you don't let them blind you or break your fingers

LXXXVI

a wonderful swinish fat one the pigs were grunting

in the end he takes tomas by the hand he'd take him to see the nice
　　brethren

they were swarming like a pack of piglets

where the released diabolical soul of the possessed had not yet been
　　embodied

tomas came back with a chestful of damson plums we spat the stones
　　out a long way off

in happy times the devil's only use was to unleash hidden treasures

a diabolical fear was shackling the hidden treasures in sandy grottos

let's nick the holy water & blind them with that water

& my wife happier & happier contemplative calm

I hope you've understood the difference between my catholic origin

& your lutheran persistence (the ogre was still smelling the blood of a
　　christian man)

anyway there's still holy water for you the only holiness is in christ
　　who no longer exists

& despite no longer existing he's left

a heap of dizzy operational sacraments

my wife was carrying on in that stunned calm of hers

then we met luciano luciani

we found him where night had left him

XC

I'm listening to tomas my mouth wide open (he's meant to be my son)
he belongs to no one as yet he still belongs to himself alone (I'm falling
    off my chair)
I won't do my homework if the teacher says I'm good I'll have to fistfight
    with everyone
if I stand up for the Pakistanis the most terroni of all terroni I'll get
    thrashed
I want to learn to play the harp become a skyblue angel on the cloud
the fireworks are done to hit christ who's up in heaven
dear daddy I know how you two made me
how long did your he-cell have to stay in mummy's she-cell?
he's puked up all of the food in the freezer & locked himself in it
I find him frozen & pissed off—to hibernate & be resurrected in a good
    thousand years
how to turn all the pages to find an ending that should be there
ever since I've been alive I've realized I'm a dog
with all the worldwide starving people they stuff me like a pig
send this food off to the starving people or I'll puke
I listen to him with my mouth wide open I fall off my chair

XCV

a relief to close the door to this room & say to myself: Now get writing!
(some shoot straight at the thing mistrusting magic)
a spectre or sorcerer was roaming around wanting vengeance
your children will be the avengers (benjamin)
he takes pleasure in the movements of his own feet
feels the joy of a god directing
the movement of his own stars from a distance
poetry as the childhood of communism
not distinguishing one's I from the revolutionary movement
it's late he keeps writing with his pen in beautiful pleasurable calligraphy
LET THOSE WHO HAVE NO POWER CAST EVERY STONE
I've walked with a hill of red ants in my mouth
among dire sufferings the wonders of the earth
this is from antonio porta too
among dire sufferings the horror of the earth
among great pleasures the glamour of the earth

XCVIII

dark-purple gleamings on the fluffy ice-cold new snow
build the angel on the new snow
lie on the new snow wave your arms again & again
the angel or angel's shadow will remain imprinted
it was calm night time suspended in that motionless still instant
I moved my bicycle
& everything started running again
on bicycle wheels
I've put Strindberg's portrait right behind my back
having to write under the possessed gaze
of my most ferocious enemy (henrick ibsen)
you're always locked in your little room it's like a pigsty
you spend your time writing don't give a damn for anything else
read the papers like a madman
recording the disasters you'll have to write about
& I must look after your children wash them iron them see to their furry
    tongues
wash cook iron dust you lock yourself in your pigsty
& come out of your pigsty like a madman with zonked-out eyes
you don't even hear what I'm saying I feel lonely depressed empty-snatched
O by the virgin mary find yourself a lover mary
I'm perfectly happy without men
can live perfectly well without your cocks
don't you touch me in fact just to spite you I got the curse as well
all my life watching this halfwit who writes & writes

& it's getting worse with time he's writing even more & getting
    even dozier
you didn't use to be this crazy you used to go out look at women
    cheat on me
you're locked in there it's not a room any more but a right pigsty
papers flying everywhere
what by the virgin mary are you chasing after with all this writing?
    where are you running to? who is calling you?

C

(among atrocious sufferings the earth's idiot)
among shameless pleasures the idiotic wonders of the earth
they're doing away with everything but the poet remained
    undaunted writing on
even on the titanic as it sank
—to write about this magic concubine
who can no longer tell herself apart from the virgin fear of death
sandpaper sanding the glass grinding the alarm-clock glass
the concept of poetry dilating to the point of falling into everything
(moribund truth keeps talking crap)
(the last humanists angry stunned hallucinating)
(in that lutheran church
I was told there was no need to redo the baptism
confirmation you have to redo concubinage too
I hope they'll get me to concubinate with another christian
that's not feasible & the usual concubine laughs)
& you little duck duckie rock the drakey duck say yes to him with
    your snow-white feathers
(when pinocchio was really good the beautiful skyblue fairy gave
    him a prize
between his legs suddenly a cock O lovely fairy)
you'll see I'll remember everything
as long as you don't whup my typewriter O lovely fairy

CIV

everything I write files in front of me pulling faces at me
this filthiest of all muses throws herself on me with all her filthy mass
she's goading me to write a nice poem against president pertini
she's attacking me with all her filthy sex I only hope she's not got
    the clap
the indispensable quality for writing is the writer's asocial attitude
happy are those who have nothing to lose who'll be able to write
    anything
& the eagle is squatting down & crying lonely out there in the frost
how I envy the marvellous gardens the beautiful floral women
the beautiful income & its wise beautiful friends
my wife says I should become a normal man
stop writing poems become a norwegic citizen
renege your Picene homeland that place near the sybillines
the beloved homeland near monfalcone appenninico with its caged
    falcon
the deboned birds & the source of the ete, lethe, perennial pure water
& pilate's lake where pilate drowned himself in those beautiful waters

CV

keep on writing anything
your behaviour must be normal
the first thing they'll ask is the precise date of the interrogation
no use telling me you've always been an antifascist
what you were yesterday will never forgive what you've become today
let's puke as far as possible
flood them with this spurted vomit
with the lightest pressure everything will spring or it should
hush little baby don't you cry papa's going to buy you a nice atom bomb
& a nice thermonuclear plant too (they're getting the rods in)
they might have got rid of their virginity
but they still get massacred with fistblows they fall off the stairs
he was about to be born as his mother sat on the toilet bowl
he was about to plummet into the bowl his bald head crowning (we are
    plummeted into the bowl)
let's put our loves into a continuous ending
you've got to draw back precisely when desire would want to incorporate
    it all
don't touch the ideology of thermonuclear plants
or everything will start exploding
here are the custodians of the sacred fire
they'll show crucifixes again when they want to crucify everyone
big fat swinelike
the pigs grunting
I was feeling good like 500 pigs

CVIII

seeing my desperate vain efforts they were laughing
& shouting you'll never make it
I was learning the new science in the original edition
everything was rushing so fast the letters were disappearing
the most delicate organ will seize up if you place it in the service of
    exploiters
with an intact brain you'll see everything & enjoy the sweetest loves
with this alphabet I feel like I've become the almighty
one word is enough & everything is printed
the pleasure of moving your legs after the plaster cast comes off
if you don't force anything everything will come sweetly & like vertigo
I thought if I managed to write beautiful poetry they'd not blind me
they killed one who was looking at the fray from the square of her
    window
on 21 september they closed the brothels aka 'houses of tolerance'
our tolerance stayed open sometimes it breaks out
there's a danger that those who got beaten up will turn terrorist the
    tolerances will explode
it seemed strange to me that even fucking
was subject to the laws of offer & demand
but I could understand very well that the relentless increase
of demand vs offer meant discount prices
could not be kept the same
she also said to me her only capital left
was that hole between her legs
they started to upturn the pots of pigswill

& it spread out quickly it was absorbed by the soil

we had to suck up the swill from the soil that was absorbing it quickly

they'll try to get us to be worse than beasts

so they can kill us without qualms as you might squash a flea between
    your nails

so here is poetry as the childhood of communism

CVIII

let's dive again into a chromatic phosphorescent nickelled fouled-up
    sea
our catastrophic poems advance over the catastrophe
—to put everything in the poems at speed throw everything out at
    speed
manage to touch that rock-hard ball with this alphabet also
in these sweetest Picene hills where this embodied alphabet was born
each letter is like the symbol of a Picene village raised over sandy
    chasms
the universe with this alphabet that can express a total universality
fingers testing these keys right left & centre
everything will be shamelessly enjoyed
joy will be delicately & protractedly at-tempted
joy would come suddenly when anguish had been at its harshest
my poem has turned into the EPP Explosive Paper Party
you'll have to atone for the sins you never even imagined you
    committed
let's see if this verbal terrorism will now break out
(papers flying out the window) you'll not manage to break my fingers
just let the thing start & it will roll on for eternity
let's spread out into entirely imaginary future times
it won't be the ferocity of terrorists & antiterrorists that stops my keys
any event by now gives a fearsome push to what I write

CXIII

it's really not enough to have killed mussolini
or mussolini's girlfriend to no longer be fascists
what you kill you will become as pavese wrote
I calmly placed myself in the grass
waiting for the landscape to absorb me
I'm spitting up the sourest gobs my stomach can no longer absorb everything
put this shitface in jail her phone bills
are getting bigger so I can't pay them any more
even in that film rats were stunned by the cretinous idiocy of men
monkeys live in shame from resembling men
& men live in shame from resembling monkeys
the american general is ready to invade the world's oil-rich lands
they'll be able to get into any place
but it's not certain they can get out
I dreamt I was trapped I really was trapped
bars clicking shut around my face
suddenly I understood why your nuts are called nuts
while the head is inside having a wonderful party
the nuts are left outside hanging around like nutcases
repression must be used while not being used by it
so as to use men they've got to reduce them to pure things
they might just stop being cannibals
out of sheer disgust for the human
in a sort of humanist antihumanism
I'm asked if I'm for or against violence
how can my for or against matter
if my only weapon is this typewriter

CXIII

the thermonuclear plants are exploding
undaunted I keep writing poems
if I fall asleep I beg you don't wake me
or I'll start writing poems again
they can give me a certificate of existence
I can do without the certificate of non-subsistence
I'll never be issued with a the certificate of good conduct
since I've not been stealing
but have paid my taxes up to the last drop of jism
I only took part in the conspiracies of invisible poetry
I cheated on my wife asking no permission
& refused to spank my children's bare bottoms
I advised my foreman to go
& get his ass fucked by a deaf donkey who'll not hear the hit
I'm in danger like a soap bubble
poetry as continual disquiet
relentless test tight sharp anguish

The Last Collection
(2002)

CXIV

I'm looking over all the letters misted over with pleasures
a night torn apart by the relentless wailing of police
they're rushing to get them save them devour them
pressure on the verses must increase so much
that the last verse will seep out of the porous casing
& Zamorra said that whenever in a church
he sees christ with wide-open arms
he thinks christ's gesture
is a save for the sins of the world
that are smashing like gunshot into the palms of his hands
& when Zamorra saves all those champions league goals
he thinks he's on an altar
& the underwritten yourstruly believes
this typewriter to be a tabernacle
the door of the holiest falls wide under a possessed hammering of keys
& there was a winter full of snow & they bombed the town
& I ran out into the country
behind my back a town was being blasted away
now & again I'd stop
to take out the snow that had soaked through my shoes
as if in all that mayhem the most important thing was
to keep my feet dry

CXVI

it's deception keeps the world fast on its hinges
certainly not the truth which is nearly always subversive
he was slamming blood & sperm everywhere
dandruff scales biological crusts
foam or snail slime
cold sore burning his lips at night
infections coming in on swallows' wings
the very evident writings that'll never be wrapped up
hermetically sealed poems that will suddenly fall wide
everything reproducing at crazy speed
even Victoria empress of the Indies a nasty coke fiend
Hitler shooting up all the time to bear with the catastrophe
only the torn apart will remain lucid

CXVIIII

the last poem inscribed with such toil
pause for breath with every word
square off with the dictionary for that hard-to-find word
everything was so luminous & intact & I felt dirty contaminated
all that snow exposed to an early sunshine
all these people exposed to death
you shall live an immortal life
only if you live continuously in the usual the obvious
those who are really alive & continuously in the unrepeatable will die
repetition the obvious the usual are timeless eternal things
those who really live are in extreme fragility
the miracle has happened the thing won't ever be repeated
as soon as it was revealed it was over for ever

CXXI

my father the mason was surely not a member of the lodge
whether pole star or southern cross
the first of the masons from Fermo to have died of lung cancer
he was convinced that even the unions were bosses' spies
he always lived in a world ordained by the enemy
he'd got old & no longer managed to grab me
he wanted to kick me but hit the wardrobe corner
with just the soft slipper protecting his poor toes
so he walked lame for a month cursing to hell
all of the poems that for good or bad I'd managed to write
for this production of verse
you need all the irresponsibility of an underwritten yourstruly
copying down the verse scrawled on urinals
top-level storms
northern lights in the strangest shapes
alcohol thermometers since the mercury ones will collapse
only the frail grasses of slopes were common property
there we would find edible herbs
we were total herbivores just like Cain
we'd slit off the thorny skins of thistles
a blunt penknife blade
our only survival tool

CXII

but for these terrible nights
I wouldn't have been able to write a line
a howl can be beautiful
but has nothing to do with art
& when you raise your voice it's difficult to understand you
they write poems as if they were great men
their legs on the ground & heads in the depths of the sky
mostly it's about optical infatuation
from the antidepressants
normally those who write poetry
are weaker than the national average
they have difficult lives full of suffering
more than giant seers
they're finches blinded in their cages
& there was no need at all
to clip their wings as well

CXXVI

I whistled to signal I was still alive
signalling my existence here I am I'm here too
in this coldest of airs as if pedalling with my genitals uncovered
the cold seemed to be turning the air to stone
the light towards the horizon was beautiful enough to tear you apart
—to die every day to have them forget we were ever alive
for those with quiet lives it's like death didn't exist
for those with screamed-out lives death really is the ultimate end
a whirlwind was reached & it's the end

CXXXII

a poet gluttonously eating stuff whether raw or cooked
unhealthy stuff too hardly chewed & gobbled up
writings only interrupted by excruciating toothaches
before long the springtime lacrimations will begin
even in the ants' headquarter we expect the sacrificing of representatives
verses with the dragon's howl stamped into them
abysmal forebodings the stolen grapes the terrorist doll
enlightened by unspeakable & unbearable frights
yet I had to face it face the mockery of comedy cretins
a frightening void how to define myself
there's no name that's not named
there was no name that wasn't terminated or animated
there were no names that weren't magnetized or contaminated
—names given things baptized propitiatory rites celebrated
even by the underwritten yourstruly who anonymously slips among
    things & papers
since everything must be titled & reconciled to the extreme
yet I was dreaming of praise of visibility
a Jew among Palestinians & Palestinian among Jews
a terror or terrone as I became in Milan
infallibly focused thick-haired as I was
shining in the dark lousy to my eyelashes

CXXXVII

scan all of your rage into the rhythm
—to speak with ferocious calm
each verse I've been able to write
—to put a chasm between me & them
or to read as if utopia
had remained only in my verse
—to act obscene in front of the whole audience
have a good time anyway
poetry is like universal blood
we can give it to anyone
but any other blood
puts us in mortal danger

CXXXIX

he shows me his school report what could I expect
from the son of such an Italian poet of the least illustrious type
her periods had disappeared for years
as soon as I dropped the condoms she got pregnant
one egg had remained undaunted waiting for life & resurrection
for a while I stopped my contest with verse
everything seemed too enormous
to be locked in the coffin of four lines of poetry laid crosswise
today the great rain beats on the glass panes
the ticking of the rain & the many keystrokes
swooping on the syllables
the wife is upbeat says I shouldn't take it so badly
we've at least been born think of the many who can't even be born
& I breathe all of your air
joyfully we were embracing

CXLI

we were loved as if swathed in God's warm breath
skyblued avenues welcomed me like wide-open vaginas
a laughing anguish auscultating everything
in identification
with this century's most sinister revolutions
existential chaos was the explosion of our joy
it's as if we were continually about to end & be perpetuated in eternity
a scapegoat sought in our abyss
all these poems inscribed
gestures without a purpose gestures
ETERNAL!

CXLIII

the anguish of being like everyone else
the opposite anguish of never being able to be like everyone else
forever cast into the role of the village idiot
the horror of enduring without any ultimate way out
—to take your first steps to escape screaming from the laughing mother
the fear of losing everything
& that everything might stick to us for ever
the most idiotic thing shameful epistles
& no longer being able to lock everything
into a suitcase & leave for ever
—to get stuck for ever in the usual shame
to get locked in the box of a stuck lift
locked alive in the coffin box

CXLIV

in a short agony then naked inside a fridge
& well frozen inside the coffin
(as per Nordic praxis) Adrian has tested it already
he'll easily be able to take my dentures out of my mouth
the final death will happen a week after I'm deceased
as soon as cremated he'll be flying
not even the underwritten yourstruly was allowed
to leave this life alive
the toilsomely inscribed mass
will finally be deciphered
so as to persist in the acts of a ritual
that will strengthen the greed for life
keep the final hour away
propitiate our joy

CLI

this universe is aching with the lust for self-knowledge
wondering about the fundamental law of the universe
they're aching for monotheism & unity
it's in these rectangular particles
that we're sentenced to know who we are
verse on sperm because the guy believes
that using an unusual lexicon
is the only way to write unusual poems
different cults still endure
men are mowed down by insecticides
this universe has proven impossible for me to internalize
multinationals i.e. kosmokrator pantokrator kyrios
the secret powers
should be annihilated at a stroke by revelation
poet i.e. krammakrator kryptokrator
all is rushing towards despair
or the other way round
what's certain is we're rushing

CLIV

you need a more than ordinary fantasy
writing in an extreme & paradoxical way
nightmares & hallucinations have become
the most realistic forms of reality
the Palestinians must be blindfolded
all of a sudden the Palestinians were swooped upon
by the bible with all of the chosen people
a hope nursed for over two thousand years swooped on the Palestinians
we were totally unprepared for so much glory
the tragedy of poetry
is that it must be an unmasking
& must use this language
which is nearly always a mask
innocence is not a gift
normally we're all killers & killers' accomplices
poetry is our soul in the face of death

CLX

I'm at ease in this life
not even the magpies let alone the idiots
will have the honour to spoil my joy of living
institutions should not multiply beyond the necessary
not even if blessed by a pius twelve
who blessed even the pigeons
& even the clay pigeon shooters were blessed
every moral duty towards animals
being considered heretical
even unescorted cars are blessed
but never cats or snakes not even when not striped
as for pussies absolutely not ever

CLXV

snowed-down snowflakes right left & centre
thoughts that kept getting disorganized
a chaos that can be inscribed
just because Mary is tidying up the scatter of papers
where the face of a barbed-wire God can be revealed
he told himself onanism is bad literature
imagining poems are written with his cock
that intruded into every hole left uncovered
poetry being
one of the many ways of seeing the world you live in
one of the many ways of putting up with it

CLXVI

to avoid that first encounter
I needn't have plummeted head down from skyscrapers
or plunged in handcuffs into river ice
or bought a second-hand electric chair & installed it in the bedroom
one shifted line of verse would have sufficed or the mirror breaking
or the favourite watch ending up in the trash
or Mary staying home to kill the cockroaches
that filled her bra & panties drawer
instead she rushed out terrified by the fear of not meeting me
& she didn't even know I existed & was waiting for her
certain as I was that nothing would ever come my way

CLXXXV

we are not destined to a long & spectacular agony
not for us the insult of being alive with no consciousness
no best-known clinicians
will set us up for long agonies of tearing pain
our poverty saves us
from the insult of being alive without our spirit left
we'll calmly return to the nothingness we came from
lucky enough that the miracle of my existence happened
I was even able to bear witness to you all

CLXXVII

here you can find the underwritten yourstruly cycling everywhere
in the evenings dead calm under the triangle of lamp light
busy listing the evils of the world
your smells & the play of your shadows behind him
on the new clean keyboard without the least speck of dust
one keystroke one clean keystroke is enough to erase the horror
or you might find me exposed stammering out my verses
in a turnal threeturnal quadriturnal night

CLXXX

he got tongue-tied about Andreotti
handed out off-course notes to passers-by
repeated with grim insistence stroke me all over
take me like a tom or randy pussycat
he'd feel up nurses & assistants
rave about supposed galactic derangements
with hugely sad gestures he'd complain
that he'd been tossed onto the most idiotic of all planets
demanding a religion
for the salvation of lost souls

CLXXXIII

a web of improper or even non-existing words
or words that turn up shamelessly for the first time
or that only I had the nerve to include
the sinking into the mirror or overflowing from the window
the drivel of a crowd of strangers
where a quiet life would be the most appropriate
a period of compulsory castration & lobotomy
& no one noticing how far we'd been brutalized
he kills his son because the world prepared for him is dire
& cannot be lived in without a radical brutalization
then he also met a bad end
two nails stuck into his head
thrown into the quicklime vat
& never identified

CLXXXVIII

if the magnetic needle could think
it would believe itself totally free
when through all eternity it's been pointing to the north pole
& any impediment to such perennial pointing
would be considered the most atrocious tyranny
so I get up on every prescribed morning at 4.30 in the morning
like nothing's the matter & I head for the factory for hell
whoever is truly oppressed can only express oppression
the torturer wants the tortured to recognize his master
in maximum security prisons I'd write my jailors' poems
I gesticulate in the most inept way
to save myself from maximum brutalization
I dreamt I was locked in a plummeting lift
& at the end of the plummeting
the lift throws me precisely onto the shop floor
clearly there was nothing left any lower down
a whole diabolical eternity left for devils to cross
those who hope look at the sky those who no longer do look at
    the floor
God created all these peoples for the fun of wasting them all
no one wondered why she was always locked in the house
the doors bolted up spying our sunsets
from the shutters' slats
& every day despaired as she noted
that we were still all there
& salvation was impossible

CXC

rivers they're no longer Eraclitus'
the riverrun water will come back & run over you more & more toxic
the planet is hermetically sealed like the aquarium for the last carp
the breathed air you'll breathe it all over again ever more polluted
totally locked horizons no use for therapies of light
of all life forms let's hope it's the cats who hold out the longest
to hold out in the caustic soda factory you need
iron health I was made of flesh & collapsed
of this near-extinct century we've seen almost all
in the morning no one will stop me getting a hit of Maria Teresa Ruta
at night a breathless search for the scariest thriller
reported for gbh because of the family situation
run over she collapses & raises from the coma with her spleen twisted out
a century with the absolute record of relentless revolutions &
    counter-revolutions
in honour of a symmetrical history with the due annihilation
anyway for good or bad this universe
has only us as its consciousness
whether aggregated or scattered till the end

CXCIII

catwalk & the starving models
their teeth gnashing sharp
moonstruck eyes & their little moues
they were told not to speak with their mouths
what they were saying with their eyes
if the mouth laughs the eyes must be ghostly
split your face in two all must be in contrast
to tell different stories with different parts of the body
arms like a little saint's & legs spatchcocked
having to show yourself a saint & whore in the same dream
projected out towards radiant futures
swallowing tapeworm to get thin
girls to get to the maximum success
you must move closest to death
come on release yourselves rebel against their enforced fastings!
sink your teeth into whole hogs with all their hairy scratchings!

CIC

months without speaking to each other
but orgasms kept bursting out undaunted
not even after the facts happened was I able to prophesize them
then the days suddenly started getting longer again
all over again fights angry bouts unransomed nightmares
the naked models sweetly let themselves be fertilized
bitching out verse became nice & tasty again
& maybe I'll be impotent with any woman
& national holidays will only be possible with Mary
the last present-arms will only be possible with Mary
& life will be able to snuff itself out at a stroke over a coitus interruptus
the best verse had been written
when there was no more reason to write it
on my bicycle I slice across the slopes of Oslo whistling
the main theme of Paganini's first violin concerto
do you know it? try to whistle it pay yourselves back

CCVI

what bothers me most is not even I
will be present at my own funeral
I at least should have been there
having constantly dragged the underwritten yourstruly
through the roughest roads in the world

CCXV

savaged by three rottweilers she'd been caring for feeding & washing
the snow & the cold upset the sequence of events
the funeral directors meant to retrieve the poor remains were blocked
in the vatican a total absence of cats & dogs
only a nesting of sacred rats
in the fattest most sanctified corners

CCXVI

I read in bed smoking & continually rearranging my position between
    the sheets
noting that the time of our death has been notified
all the ideas I get in my head come through the sheets
even in Milan people were beginning to shed their overcoats
supporting Napoli doesn't yet include widespread murder
in a faithfulness made fast by the terror of a return of the crabs
or of falling back into beds full of cockroaches
incapable as I am of putting up with the crunching of chased-out
    woodworm
the mothballs scattered by the wife
even in my shirt pockets
little clouds of mosquitoes on the windowsill plants
the bee gently taken by the wings
& exported out the window
so as not to commit any useless murders

CCXVII

as if in the whole universe in absolute darkness
the sudden illumination of our consciousness had happened
just to plunge everything back into absolute blindess
this is the only life we have at our disposal
let's get supreme existence out of our head we are alone & desperate
with swindlers whether mitred or not profiting off our anguish
calmly accept the anguish of no longer having an eternal father
as at ever-increasing speed the end of the species approaches
the dinosaurs are finished now the hourglass is upended for humans
all the tarmacs will be filled with new grass
anthills & beehives will spring up in the most unpredictable places
new teeming of earwigs under every stone
no one will find any trace of our existence

CCXIX

an infinity wide open on all sides
a nothing is enough to save the world
a spot-on verse is enough to save the day
like when masses of warm & cold air
are in perfect balance
& a flutter of wings on the wrong side
is enough to cause the catastrophe
everything will be worse than we might have imagined
the days will get shorter & shorter until total darkness
& we'll not be able to give up
we were making up new conspiracies
we'll not be able to write
unless threatened by a fearsome sickness
a world with infinite worlds & we are birthing
infinite ones relentlessly because an infinity
always has space for a new infinity
despite the brevity of our life
which just to spite us is also unrepeatable

CCXXV

I should convince myself to live like I were dead
shut myself up in a diving suit
& well deformed well protected face the horror of the obvious
& so I wound up in the cemetery in Pisa
with a geometric & ceremonious paradise
& a hell in the chaos with satan in the most desperate hunger
the implacable representation of social horror
brushed & brutalized by each & every doubt
the fly in the spiderweb who by struggling
makes the threads of the trap all the more inescapable over us
doubt tearing you apart for a poem that'll never be published
the pen slipping between my fingers from the sweating
& we were not able to give up
anyway no struggling for breath
let's preserve ourselves a long time in this calm destitution
as we try to reach the ultimate revelation
the ultimate spasm

CCXXVIII

the glass panes are glassed over with glassy frost
my plasma is glassed over the mirror
the flowers of a botanic glass pane
that will disappear with the sweet warm breaths of spring
& all this anguish to be written
catch your breath organize yourself with every word
revolutionary mysticism or subversive christianity
that desperate eye tearing our hope apart
a catastrophe in the anthill
where they pour petrol & set fire to it all
the queen will manage to escape with singed wings
this joy of being alive will not be repeated

CCXXXIV

as I get out of the car two policemen approach me
one asks for my papers & they start rummaging
& search the car as well
they find a harmless little penknife in my pocket
start slapping me around giving no reason
in the meantime a second police car arrives
I end up in handcuffs
charged with insult to public officer
no matter that I'd said nothing
& meekly let myself be slapped about
taken to the police station they resume the beating
two broken ribs
16-day prognosis for severe abrasive trauma
I report the facts
a court clerk tells me I've been lucky
you should be thankful they didn't throw you out the window

CCXXXV

those who have seen my childhood are all dead by now
today I took my youngest child to school
he goes to a catholic school
with the children of refugees from all over the world
from Vietnam anticommunists to Chilean communists' kids
the year-one teacher is a nun she hugs them all
a little magazine printed in one copy full of positive news
she managed to cycle along the edge of the low wall along the
    new road
undaunted by the double chasms
a wall just about two-feet wide
sheer from the small tower
with its one-hand clock all the way
the steps that saw
all of our speculations on times & spaces
& even the fluttering of bats around lampposts
had to disappear for ever
the world of desolate nights inescapably approaching
no honeymoon bury me in unconsecrated ground
far from the Christian feral beasts let's disincarnate in peace
we are hounded by a joyful complex
the sweetest tangerines from Grottammare
submerged in the early snow
a snow that turned to water as soon as held in your fists
a whiteness ready to come undone
in the early flavour of a dawn like any other

CCXLVII

you couldn't tell what was dirtier the holy water from the stoup
or the drinking water all infected yet the last time
flying over the alps on an Alitalia plane
I saw all that snow shining in the sun so shamelessly beautiful
much snow had turned grey as if grown old
but much of it was white & unsullied so much of it
even the curly haired girl had her nose glued to the window
the wing was vibrating dangerously then we started going down
    towards Oslo
I could see a whole poem as seen by an Icarus
thrown from this height
the flaming of many a whiteness
purest pillars in earlier & earlier becoming
I was throbbing & plummeting endlessly
gripped with no respite by a deranging whiteness

CCLIX

poems by a young poet
read by an old man with a wobbly denture
they were unrecognizable the firefighters in the flames
managing to find a completely naked young man
& the amateur pyro shoots himself in the mouth as soon as they
    find him
despite being prey to the flames
look for the definite ending at all costs
he took no drugs didn't run after girls
his mother who'd tried to calm him down
got a faceful of bad bruises
he tries to knife himself douses the living-room furniture in petrol
what shall I do kill myself?
kill my wife's mother & the cat as well?
what to do so as to remain faithful to myself?
what saint to turn to?
where to turn to stone?
how to end?

CCLXI

by now not even the spectre of Hamlet's father is haunting Europe
the doors are open for the swine & its enemies
anyway the means of poetic communication
are all & forever in our hands
writing is not hard at all since everything has been written on top of us
I'm sending the swine all of my esteem including the kind regards
cannot send you the underwritten yourstruly he won't fit in the envelope
they throw stones at me because they see their own sins in yourstruly
Fortini keeps writing about the servants' servants but who knows what
    he means
beautiful to live out of focus like this like they've reduced me to
but what will be the meaning of these painstaking word experiments?
I who down the centuries have spied a severely short-sighted monster
he'd take his glasses off to read & put them back on so as to stop seeing
    anything
he had incredible memory could remember all of our sins
spying on every verse every move from the typewriter keys every
    correspondence
& it will all get irretrievably ordered along continual chaos
being able by language to have anyone believe anything
& to show men up in their most shameful reality

CCLXIX

a raid under the bridges
on the streets leading to the necropolis
bishopric kitchen gardens in advanced decomposition
the show from the windows the traffic jams
car chases horns blaring the fair of transvestites
three types of huge Brazilian transsexuals with marble breasts
small knives stashed in the heels of their peep-toes
displaying their black sexes stiff as truncheons
over this whole landscape the huge anarchist graffiti
even an exclamation-mark Stalin in the background
nomads are throwing stones at the neofascist vans
this was the last lively moment
then suddenly everything died down

CCLXXII

don't leave the studio apartments empty
squatters are looking out checking obituaries
even the morgue slab is too highly priced
it's fights at knifepoint for a place under the bridges
the graveyards are overfilled with the dead
no chance they can house the living
unable as we are to keep up with the rent
thrown to the raging madness of evictions
& the ultimate doom
house the world's runtaways
in our cathedrals
make an effort
try to become christians

CCLXXVII

all the swines were forbidden to exist within the city walls
only swine corpses were allowed in
their graveyards in our bellies
any viper dog cat & the hungry lice
were given free entry
into the tangle of these mindless verses
strongholds of the last-stand resistance
the spirit of the new times could still announce itself
we demand real findings not abstract conjecture
now we can see the berlusked groups being allowed in
to keep this sort of political party going
you need tons of cocaine
all they did was scream
we was conned by the shoemaker!
& onwards snorting away
with stones dropped off of motorway bridges
crazy arrows piercing the unaware
even the switched-off phones
were broadcasting all the sinning
we did with a fearless cock
the carrier of the most deranged hopes

CCXCV

an epic of this sort would need endless electroshocks
highest-tension poetry keep off danger of death
all good things come from the sky as the drinker of rainwater said
as he saw & drank all those drops swooping hard on him
he sleeps with his eyes open so he can watch the world from sleep
poems needing the blowtorch more than the chisel
maceration in the vat of nitric acid might also work
numberless cuttings & pastings in the manuscripts of an underwritten
    yourstruly
& all must be titled & ultimately reconciled
the movement when in jail does nothing but write poems
subjected to the merciless critique from the censorship of carceral order
adulterated incitements to well-oiled class hatred & revenge
armed struggle association by portable olivetti
the irreducibility of these thin sheets
the stubborn one blacking his papers by night replicates his own error
as Fortini wrote & the groaning of glaciers under premature heats
piss turned into steaming ice
the chaster she is the more worried about the empty fridge
the artifice of rhyme & the ogre's presence
the birds stiffed around the factory vents
the sweepers swive-sweeping all around the corpses
the revolution & embodiment of all these verbs
or disembodied & taut in a spellbound gleaming

CCXCVII

so here I am aching to write
until I'm poured onto my papers
all my verse broadcast through pure contagion
all those afternoons with letters swooping down
on the paper in joyful whirlwinds
searching for the emblem of our spirit

CCCIV

the tearing pain in the factory was unspeakable
those who were inside the hell of the workers' condition said nothing
& those who were outside of it
could say anything but knew nothing
so the poet had to plunge into the daily hell
grease up his hands over forty years of aggravation
set off on his bicycle at five in the morning
even at minus twenty heading for armageddon
with furious good cheer I clock my presence in
it bears witness to the fact that even this underwritten yourstruly exists
& inscribes the verses of our epigraph

CCCXII

Sbarbaro the poet of lichens I loved so much
lichens I photograph all the time
they're in love with the corners where every other life is denied
bushing up on hostile planets

CCCXIV

coming out of the factory was like coming out of a war
it's only by chance that you come out alive
all that grease the filings from the draw bench
scorching detergents the screeching of iron
the sweat dripping into your eyes
burning its way down to your lips
this howl cannot be heard
neither could the howls of all of us together
those who can't take it will be thrown into
maximum atrocity
the factory is the last station
if you get sacked it's like you've been spat out into the unknown
in a fall that will not be cushioned
the steelworker is attached to something diabolical
the Polish man says working
for the red new dawn under the communists was even worse
some of the stopped machines look like coffins
for those who are really sick
to stay off sick is not that easy
this foreigner this Italian guy we don't know much about him
all we know is he stinks & he exists

CCCXVIII

the apartments occupied by squatters
born without licence
not very well accepted pretty badly breastfed
sulphuric dioxide corroding the national glories
binge-loads of Swiss dioxine transplanted into Italy for safety
even the worker cats are scandalized
by the suicides for the shame of Bribe City
the waters rainbowed over by the slicks of last-rites oil
here come the sandoz colouring agents
the plunging of sea birds over floating waste
a portrait fixed inside a landscape being erased
never so many crusts of bread for the entirely toothless mothers
most people were assaulted whether or not by mistake
next to the packed-up dispensing machines
waiting ten years for the pension
with a hundred percent invalidity
if I hadn't kept working in the meantime I'd have starved to death
& here I am unprepared for the final consummation
the mother under investigation with three samurai swords in her
    bedroom
next thing I know a guy fills my face with fist blows & says to me:
love thy neighbour you piece of shit!
hence perforce & per disconcerted consistency
I hereby commend my soul to
SANCTUS ANTONIUS ULYSSIPONENSIS
COGNOMINIR PATAVINUS

Lisbon having been founded by Ulysses
after which accompanied by blowing a raspberry we shall produce
    the invoking epistle
specially delivered & particularly recommended
even by the officers of the epistolary or episcopate as may be

The Laughing God

(2008)

the blind universe
was aching to see itself
in the end it managed to create the human eye
& the universe could finally see itself
then men created God

1

dark thoughts black thoughts surfacing
—to fly out the window
plunge into that cherry tree
growing outside my house
it glows
luminous through the springtides
suddenly without a warning it blossoms
clusters of joyful life
so the season starts
when no one imagines he'll have to die

2

it's no small thing
to feel like you're god's child
to know he believes in us
& in the work of the underwritten yourstruly
it's even possible
that humanity itself is God
& that each one of us is holy & sacred

6

since the day they got me born
I haven't quite been myself
I lost my intellect
& could never find it whole again
I gobble up all the chocolates & melons
all the words all the mistakes
I can't tell you where I've been
since I've not come back yet

7

the underwritten yourstruly
is a card-carrying copycat
even able to copycat still
unpublished collections

11

memorable days:
luther hangs
his 95 theses
to the door of wittenberg cathedral
meeting in st james' church
the bolshevik party
decides to go ahead with armed struggle

17

to fight the devil
you need an even more diabolical angel
to fight the angel
the devil endevils himself even more
& I couldn't exactly understand what fucking universe
I'd ended up living in
the universe being infinite there must be
a universe I've been demoted from by mistake

18

I'm a non-believer & feel full of sin
in a house whose corners
are heaped with the filthiest filth
hours & hours admiring the bad omens
that endlessly file along the walls
raging outside god's grace

25

I get up at five in the morning
a new day begins like nothing's the matter
I carry on writing until everything's as easy
as shadows lengthening & shortening
verses are bending right left & centre
sinking into the darkest places
loving everything multiplied by everything

27

I was in mortal danger
immediately I think
if I manage to wake up
I'll be saved

28

truth is expressed
by a mangled
stuck chaotic transcription
torn-apart transcription

29

O let us admire
the endless divine wisdom
which immediately understood
that without endless sexual pleasures
this most filthy human species
would never have passed itself down

31

as long as there's psychiatrists
we risk ending up toothless
as long as there's seas
no doctor need risk being tied up
as long as there's pork eaters
pigs are in danger
as long as there's cops
each one of us risks ending up in handcuffs
as long as there's a pope
there'll be the popped-open
as long as there's dogs
cats risk ending up bitten
as long as there's wedded couples
there'll be huge weary topples
as long as there's men
nature risks being devoured

33

I wish you all a happy easter
you'll eat the flesh & blood
of our lord Mr Jesus Christ
let's hope you won't
choke on a leftover bone

37

I feel you're mine as the air I breathe
I kiss your mouth
my breath rising as if I were running
& with you I enjoy
this our love
your being a natural at joy

41

on this bright morning
it's as if god himself
had come in to visit me
through the wide-open window

44

the shock you go through when you come into the world
the air icy after the warmth
of the motherly womb
the blinding light
deafening noises
poetry backtracks to the primal anguish
& we got to imagine that electroshock
would sort things out
since the initial shock
needed to be endlessly repeated

48

the doors of hell
have been barred shut for ever
you're all holy & saved
no one left in hell except chained-up devils
& at the end of all time
everything will return to God's belly
nothing will be lost
everything will be joyfully saved

58

last night I saw you all again
splendidly alive
once again we saw
all the horrors of that shop floor & we were laughing
they didn't get to kill us
we're all still alive
new as if resurrected
no longer tainted by dirty death

66

they came out of the pool hideous disgusting
I'd never seen them all in a group
I was waiting for them to come out that pool
they passed me by
patted me on the head with outstretched hands
the whiffs of chlorine
it was like the stench of hell
& if I bathe in that water
I'll become like them

88

a chaos of christs & madonnas
with the chance that a heavenly body
or a luminous comet will fall on us
& we all suddenly end up blinded
I who on account of a furious eros was half devoured
by crabs big as canine elephants

93

& they're signalling to me to get a move on
I shouldn't be the one missing
I leave it said they'll have to cremate me right away
my ashes to be placed
between my parents'
so I'll disappear back where I came from

106

with your shadow shifting
towards the last ruin for some time now
but if you look carefully below you
the seagulls
are all flying with lit-up wings

108

my father was a bricklayer
& whenever I see a church wall
I don't think of God
but of bricklayers & of my father
& now it's my turn to become a father
after being too long a son
my identity unrepeatable
like the small light signals
about to disappear for ever

109

I like to walk barefoot around the house
the wife scatters
drawing pins all over the floor
to punish my bad habit
but I'm hopping about holding out

123

on seeing myself suddenly
in the mirror
I got scared
as if I'd been faced
with someone wanting to murder me

129

I'm terrified at the mere thought
of being kept alive if totally paralysed
in the absolute darkness of unconsciousness
enforced treatment is terrifying
the worst thing is not dying
but living as if dead

132

So Giancarlo tells me he'll invite me
to read my poems at the poetry house in Milan
only when I turn 90
if so then I'll invite myself to read poems in hell
if so then he'll have to pay my round-trip
since I don't wish to remain trapped for ever
with the poets of our poetry's capital city

133

by now I'm a poet who shovels northern snow
it's very light snow at minus ten
snow like the lightest of feathers
floating in the snow-white airs
by now we should consider the underwritten yourstruly
as one in the underworld sending
reckless relentless messages

my grandmother's house
was teeming with roaches
one had sunk to the bottom of a coffee cup
& ended up in my mouth
I spat it out with extreme violence
& really did wrong the cockroach being
the symbol of eternity
& it was eternity falling into my mouth

So I meet Mary in an alley in Oslo
she gets pregnant right away
with a catastrophe of crabs an invasion of roaches
& we delved unawares into happy relentless derangements
& though she's never read
even one line of the poems I've written
she suggests lines to me all the time
& I take them apart & put them back again
so as to happily reach
the madness of all things

143

I could no longer control myself
under the tent I had a mattress
full of land mines & dynamite
several weapons for sabotage & terrorism
the guy meant to collaborate with me
did nothing but explain the situation to me in Finnish
I couldn't understand a word
of his relentless stammering
it was raining & thundering
& water was beginning to seep in everywhere
so much so that in the end
we couldn't even blow ourselves up

149

normally I'm an atheist
but sometimes I believe in God
some other times I can feel a universe
devoid of God's existence
& my happiness is total
that's God himself
loving his own non-existence

150

mary too had got lost
I was trying to find her
if she exists you'll find her more or less banged up
onto an eternal page
where procreation having made way
for resurrection
balls will have become pitifully useless

poetry has never made me a penny
the underwritten yourstruly's poetry
is a disinterested gesture
gifted free of charge to all men
including women in love
preferably fat women who are more cheerful
less gloomy less desperate than the thin ones
since they've got to go
through a whole lifetime laughing

181

a night lit up
only by the headlight of my bike
and on the shortcut across the park
on the new snow
I suddenly spied a cat's footprints
it was as if a shadow were sliding by
a swift black cat on the immaculate snow
please if you don't want to come to a bad end
fly away from Chinese restaurants
they love the seventh meat
they're looking for the Nordic tiger
your phosphorescent eyes

183

all of a sudden I understood
that God is nothing but
an idealization of the boss
even dogs have bosses
& believing in God
does not really set us aside from dogs
with bosses gone
God too would be gone behind the bend
& we'd be told apart from dogs

190

all of a sudden you find yourself
facing the 24 / 25 December utterly unprepared
shaken by the pealing of bells
facing a tree all ribboned up with little gold stars
where has all this stardust come from?
who might have wanted me to exist?
who might have insisted so that my existence
would be believed to be so necessary?
why was it precisely me
who had to live inside this guy luigi di ruscio?

We are all equal in front of the law, but I'm more equal than others. This sentence is not by Silvio Berlusconi but by the pig in the 'animal farm' as written by George Orwell.

my mouth is full of butterflies
I know full well if I open my mouth
they'll all fly away
& won't come back even
if I keep my mouth wide open for ever

213

the underwritten yourstruly a total poet
having used his intelligence only to write poems
needed no more than his idiocy to live among you all
brawn for sale
brain kept as exclusive private property
in the service of a dream

216

deep night
I look up towards the fluttering
of the wafers of snow
dazzled by this
splendid eucharist
that covers everything
makes everything holy

218

it's five in the morning
we're surrounded by a deafening silence
I can see all things coming at me
something excruciating is bursting out everywhere
it is possible to report everything to you
since by sheer chance I'm still in this life

225

the games against myself I always lose them all
& mary keeps yelling at me
that I'd better get normal
stop writing poems
become a Norwegian citizen
but stubbornly I
persist in the horror

235

I saw a cat with her kittens
no sooner birthed than she'd eaten them
& I started on becoming a poet for ever

253

all of a sudden the underwritten yourstruly
gets a glimpse of God's smile
of God's mercy
& even God's joy
beginning to laugh like a madman
finding myself whole inside the grace of God
quiet enjoyment of his joy
since we men are God's creators
each of us having the God he deserves

265

it wasn't the airborne down from plants
that caused my allergic attacks
our dwelling was exhaling unbearable pain
excrement & liquid trash scattered everywhere
& that little girl smiling at us
despite having been thrown
into the centre of our hell

269

my homeland is all in my memory
childhood friends I meet them they smile
out of the photographs in our graveyards' niches
my homeland pared down to the Italian language
to what can live anew in these verses
in these deranged papers
half-blinded by the TV mouth
with an underwritten yourstruly deranged by hallucination
& entirely unequal to the task of recording the world's grief

274

my father would write poems just like mine
he told me he lost all his teeth spat them out
& he was laughing

277

these last few years I've been
seized by short short
rapid-fire poems
most violent poems
in real time with no subterfuge

I only use Italian to write
my daily language is Norwegian
Italian almost becomes a dead language
real people including the whole of the underwritten yourstruly
become characters in a dream
opening up a gaping chasm
with tooth-broken flesh-gashed poems
as if spat out well spread
over people's faces

285

the miracle is that we're alive
like the marvellous soap bubbles
one instant before disappearing
it is our life's extreme precariousness
that gives a sacred character to our existence

armies of giant mosquitoes
followed by roof-wrecking rains
I was whistling all the time in the vain attempt
to tell everyone I was also there
with all my verse being deciphered only
by the accomplices in our poetic conspiracy
even when there was a blackout
& we bumped into each other we were laughing
then everything was back as it was before
& again we saw in one another's faces the usual ferocity

294

I knew full well that going against your conscience
is most dangerous especially for me
who ride around everywhere on a bicycle
you risk a catastrophe on the tarmac like nothing's the matter
risk a brain tumour like nothing's the matter
insomnias & loss in a relentless hell

305

lengthy amorous manoeuvring & then the swift orgasm
just like poems with manoeuvres of all kinds
& suddenly when you least expect it
here comes our poem

hope must be shown immediately
no use keeping it hidden
lest it be stolen
support it with blasphemous or spherical verses
& at the end of your compositions
as if slamming the lid
of a coffin
close everything

Translator's Notes

A NOTE ON THE TEXT: I have chosen to respect the erratic capitalization in the original and translate the few intended lapsus words as closely as possible. Neither did I feel at liberty to edulcorate or explain away any expressions that current convention may deem problematic or offensive.

PAGE 24 | **Picene**: derived from Picenum, the ancient name of the Italian area where the Marche region is situated.

PAGE 28 | **'red brand red heartland shining'**: in the original, 'e brillava la marca rossa', where 'marca' refers both to the red brand name of the cheap 'Popolari' cigarettes from the State monopoly and to the communist sympathies of part of the 'Marca', a toponym sometimes used for 'Marche'.

PAGE 46 | *L'Unità*: the official broadsheet of the Italian Communist Party until 1991.

PAGE 48 | *Giornale d'Italia*: a right-wing newspaper founded in 1901, and published until 1976.

PAGE 58 | **Morra**: a hugely popular hand game dating back to Roman times.

PAGE 67 | **Giuseppe Morichetti**: a scholar from Fermo and one of the founders in 1959 of the State Archive situated in the town.

PAGE 114 | **Bruno Barilli**: a composer from the Marche who wrote extensively about music.

'say the age of Christ': a reference to the word 'trentatré' (thirty-three), which some doctors asked their patients to pronounce during auscultation.

PAGE 116 | **Santa Caterina**: the parish in Fermo where Di Ruscio was born, and of the church in the town dedicated to St Catherine of Alexandria.

PAGE 119 | **'cross of all delights'**: a détournement of the Italian expression 'croce e delizia', usually denoting a person, object or situation regarded as a source of both trouble and enjoyment.

PAGE 122 | **Loreto Litany**: a prayer to the Virgin Mary traced back to the 13th century, also to the sanctuary in the town of Loreto in the Marche.

PAGE 123 | **'in genoa laid out'**: a reference to the brutality meted out on a massive scale by police during the G8 demonstrations in Genoa in July 2001, including acts of torture against protesters and the death of 23-year-old Carlo Giuliani at the hands of an officer.
'eight signatures': a flashback reference to the eight referendums proposed by the Radical Party in the '70s.

PAGE 124 | **'O fair stars of the Bear… the Firman firmament'**: the constellation in Leopardi's canto expands and then collapses in the starry sky over Di Ruscio's hometown, Fermo.

PAGE 133 | **'how salt is the taste'**: a reference to the *Divine Comedy* (Paradiso XVII) in which one of Dante's ancestors foretells the poet's exile.

PAGE 136 | **'correspondence of loving senses'**: an ironic take on a line from Ugo Foscolo's *Sepulchres*.

PAGE 147 | **Davide Lazzaretti** (1834–78): a Tuscan preacher who founded a mountain community based on a form of mystical socialism. Initially supported by church authorities as a foil to the expansion of a secular State, Lazzaretti was later excommunicated. A procession he had organized was intercepted by a police squad, and he was shot down along with three of his followers.

PAGE 149 | **'roversi writes'**: the poet Roberto Roversi (1923–2012); a partisan during the Italian Resistance, he was a co-founder of *Officina* and for some time the director of the news sheet *Lotta Continua*. Roversi chose to publish his poetry outside the mainstream and to continue his work as a cultural activist from the bookshop he and his wife Elena Marcone had opened in Bologna in 1948 and ran until 2006.

'barbsqueak': in the original, 'sgarrotti sbarbini', possibly a pun on the name of a prominent Italian literary critic.

'sanguineti was right': Edoardo Sanguineti (1930–2010), the poet, critic and founding member of neoavanguardia Gruppo '63.

'quasimodo wrong': the poet Salvatore Quasìmodo (1901–68), whose *Letter to Mother*, to which Di Ruscio is referring here, uses the vocative 'mater dolcissima' ('gentlest', or literally, 'sweetest' mother), mixing the Latin of church invocations to the Virgin Mary with ordinary speech.

'when reading croce': Benedetto Croce (1866–1952), the philosopher and critic whose liberal and anti-totalitarian teachings had a deep influence on Italian culture and politics.

PAGE 150 | 'soul of the possessed': from the episode in the New Testament (Mark 5:1–20) in which Jesus casts demons out of a man's body into a herd of pigs which then rush into the sea and are drowned.

Luciano Luciani: a carpenter and friend of the poet's.

PAGE 150 | 'most terroni of all terroni': a disparaging term used to refer to southern Italians (from 'terra': soil, earth, land).

PAGE 152 | 'from antonio porta too': Antonio Porta (1935–89) was a literary and theatre critic, poet and a member of the neoavanguardia. He was among the first to recognize Di Ruscio's work, and included him in his seminal anthology *Poesia italiana degli anni Settanta* (Milan: Feltrinelli, 1979). Porta and Di Ruscio exchanged letters over a number of years.

PAGE 156 | 'poem against president pertini': Sandro Pertini (1896–1990), the antifascist politician who served as the president of the republic from 1978 to 1985.

'near the sybillines': the Monti Sibillini, a massif sited between the Marche and Umbria regions, part of the Apennines range that runs the length of the Italian peninsula.

'ete, lethe': in the original, a pun on the toponyms of one of the rivers local to Di Ruscio's hometown (the Ete) and that of the Lethe, the underworld river of oblivion in Greek and Roman mythology ('Lete' in Italian).

'pilate's lake': Lago di Pilato, a lake in the Monti Sibillini that owes its name to the belief that Pontius Pilate drowned in its waters.

PAGE 158 | 'square of her window': a reference to Teresa Ricciardi, a woman shot dead by police in 1969 while watching from her balcony as worker's and students' protests unfolded in the streets of Battipaglia, in the Campania region.

PAGE 165 | '& Zamorra said': refers to Ricardo 'El Divino' Zamora (1901–78), a famous Spanish goalkeeper.

PAGE 179 | 'blessed by a pius twelve': Pope Pius XII was head of the Catholic Church from March 1939 until his death in October 1958.

PAGE 187 | Maria Teresa Ruta: is an Italian TV celebrity.

PAGE 195 | 'kosmokrator, pantokrator, kyrios' (literally 'ruler of the universe', 'ruler of all', 'lord'): titles originally given to Christ that Di Ruscio sees as blasphemously incorporated by capital in its lust for power. He responds to this by a Shelleyan micro-manifesto for the underground poet, who rules by writing ('krammakrator', where 'kramma' is a lapsus or possibly an intentional alliterative assimilation for 'grámma') and in hiding ('kryptokrator').

PAGE 198 | Grottammare: is a town on the Marche coast, south of Fermo.

PAGE 204 | 'the berlusked groups': in the original text the word 'berluscati' (derived from Berlusconi) refers to the Italian tycoon turned politician who was at the centre of numerous political, sexual and financial scandals during and after his intermittent tenure as prime minister between 1994 and 2011.

'the shoemaker': Diego Della Valle, a businessman in the footwear industry from the Marche region who was vocal in accusing Berlusconi of failing to support business. Hence the 'berlusked groups' purporting to have been 'conned by the shoemaker'.

PAGE 208 | 'Sbarbaro the poet of lichens I loved so much': Camillo Sbarbaro (1888–1967), the Ligurian poet who was also an internationally renowned lichenologist.

PAGE 210 | 'Bribe City': from 'Tangentòpoli', the name given to the system of corruption implicating Italian finance and politics exposed in the early '90s by an inquest known as Many Pulite (Clean Hands).

'crusts of bread for the entirely toothless mothers': an ironic take on the Italian proverb according to which 'those who have bread lack the teeth'.

PAGE 242 | 'So Giancarlo tells me': the Milanese poet Giancarlo Majorino (1928–2021), whose first publication was titled *La capitale del nord* (The Northern Capital City).

Translator's Acknowledgements

During translation work on the incredible anarchitecture of Luigi Di Ruscio's poetry, I had the good fortune to be in conversation with Angelo Ferracuti, and to enjoy the warm hospitality of the home he shares with his wife, Alessandra Tortato: heartfelt thanks to them both for making this possible.

Special thanks also to Andrea Cavalletti and Massimo Gezzi for supporting this project, Angelo Giavatto for the devil in the philological detail, and to the European Literature Network for publishing two of the poems from this collection in their review (*The Italian Riveter*, April 2022).

Summer 2023